# RichThoughts
## for Breakfast
### Volume 7

*Harold Herring*

President of The Debt Free Army
& RichThoughts TV

www.HaroldHerring.com

Debt Free Army
PO Box 900000, Fort Worth, TX 76161

RichThoughts for Breakfast Volume 7
by Harold Herring

ISBN: 978-0-9763668-8-1
Copyright © 2019 by the Debt Free Army
PO Box 900000, Fort Worth, TX 76161
817-222-0011
harold@haroldherring.com

Unless otherwise noted, Scripture references are taken from the King James Version of the Bible.

# RichThoughts for Breakfast
## Volume 7
## Table of Contents

# What Makes You the
# Head and Not the Tail

As I was praying this morning … the Lord's direction was very clear. He gave me six questions to ask you … then a scripture and an exhortation.

How did you see yourself as a *child?*

How did you see yourself in *high school and college?*

How did you see yourself in *athletic or academic endeavors?*

How did you see yourself *with members of the opposite sex?*

How did you see yourself *in the marketplace?*

How did you see *yourself in marriage and with a family?*

Truthfully, I should *probably change the word "did" in all these sentences to the word "do"* … because the real question … right now … is **how DO you see**

**yourself today and more importantly, tomorrow?**

*If there is one message that I seek to continually convey in meetings, seminars, letters, blogs, television and internet programs … it's encouraging believers to see themselves the way God sees them because that changes everything.*

Deuteronomy 28:13 says:

> *"And the LORD shall make thee the head, and not the tail; and thou shalt be above only, and thou shalt not be beneath; if that thou hearken unto the commandments of the LORD thy God, which I command thee this day, to observe and to do them."*

Remember these words were first used on slaves … *walking in a slave mentality … coming up out of Egypt.* They were *used as an example for us* … according to I Corinthians 10:11 that *we might escape the bondages of slavery they experienced* and *know how to enter our Promised Land, the abundant life Jesus redeemed us for.*

**First, get ahold of this … THE LORD SHALL MAKE THEE.** Not anybody else, the Lord … our great God Jehovah … Elohim, the Almighty One <u>shall make you</u>.

<u>We're not talking about an assistant to an assistant … even an angel … God, your Heavenly Father will make YOU</u>.

<u>The head</u> and not the tail.

That's the exhortation … that's the word God wanted me to share with you this morning.

You're the head and not the tail … then He said … tell my children to act like who they are during the next year.

According to Strong's Concordance the Hebrew word for head is ro'sh (rrow sush) and it means:

> **"head, top, summit, upper part, chief, total, sum, height, front, beginning, choice, best."**

**The head is a position of leadership.**

The *tail* according to Strong's Concordance means *"the end of something."*

**God's plan is to make you the chief … the choice … the best … the total of all that is.** He never intended for you to be the end of a thing.

Colossians 2:10 in the New Living Translation says:

> *"So you also are complete through your union with Christ, who is the head over every ruler and authority."*

Get ready to shout as we read Deuteronomy 28:13 in the New Living Translation which says:

> *"If you listen to these commands of the Lord*

*your God that I am giving you today, and if you carefully obey them, the Lord will make you the head and not the tail, and you will always be on top and never at the bottom."*

I want you to pay particular attention to the last eleven words in that verse. Let's read them again.

*"You will always be on top and never at the bottom."*

God's desire for you is so clear … He wants you to be the chief … the leader who is always on top … winning in the game of life.

**The key to manifesting His desire for you … is the same as it was for the children of Israel … <u>listen and obey</u>.** *Listening and obeying His Word places you in the position to receive all good things.*

*"If you listen to these commands of the Lord your God that I am giving you today, and if you carefully obey them."*

If we obey His Word … if we follow His instructions … then all these things will happen to us.

2 Timothy 2:20-21 in the New Living Translation says:

*"So whoever cleanses himself [from what is ignoble and unclean, who separates himself from contact with contaminating and corrupting influences] will [then himself] be a vessel set apart*

*and useful for honorable and noble purposes, consecrated and profitable to the Master, fit and ready for any good work."*

**Are you ready for every good work?**

***Okay, God tells you to stop it!*** **Stop looking at where you're at … and begin focusing on where you can and will be through obedience.**

No one is deserving of His grace, so stop putting your imperfection or lack of talent in the equation.

The really good news is that *if you start on the bottom or even if you feel like you're starting on the bottom …* you don't have to stay there.

1 Corinthians 7:20-23 in the New Living Translation says:

*"Yes, each of you should remain as you were when God called you. Are you a slave? Don't let that worry you—but if you get a chance to be free, take it. And remember, if you were a slave when the Lord called you, you are now free in the Lord. And if you were free when the Lord called you, you are now a slave of Christ. God paid a high price for you, so don't be enslaved by the world."*

Truly, God did pay a very high price for us. He sacrificed His only begotten Son that you and I might have life eternal and abundantly.

So make no mistake about it ... **God doesn't want you to be in bondage at all and** *He most definitely doesn't want you to stay in bondage* ... financial or otherwise.

**God wants you free**. *Say that with me. "God wants me to be free."* Say it again and this time personalize it by adding your name. "God wants Harold Herring to be free."

One more thing ... *it doesn't matter what you've experienced in the past ... loss, financial or personal, embarrassment or disappointment. It's not where you're at or what you were doing when God called you ...* when He chose you to be the head and not the tail ... to be above and not beneath.

**Through your obedience to His instructions ... you will rise to spiritual and natural prominence.**

You may not have felt or even feel now that you're smart enough to be the leader God wants you to be ... but truthfully, *what He thinks about you is much more important than what you think about yourself* ... at the moment.

1 Corinthians 1:26

*"Remember, dear brothers and sisters, that few of you were wise in the world's eyes or powerful or wealthy when God called you."*

**God has the unique ability to make something out**

**of nothing and that's what He'll do with you … if you just let Him.**

Just remember your journey to the top … begins and ends with your obedience to His commands.

James 1:25 in the Contemporary English Version says:

> *"But you must never stop looking at the perfect law that sets you free. God will bless you in everything you do, if you listen and obey, and don't just hear and forget."*

If we listen and obey … *God will bless us in everything we do* … regardless of what we had and where we started on our journey.

**Wow … what an incredible promise … if you listen and obey you will be blessed.**

*Grasp these truths until you are able to freely walk in them. God is not talking about someone else … He's talking about His children and that includes YOU!*

# Day 2

## 7 Things to Do Today

I made a list of seven thought-provoking ... *life-changing keys*. <u>I'm going to share them with you</u>.

Make a list of how God has blessed you. I want to say that again ... because I want to make sure ... **you're taking notes and writing this down**.

First ... *make a list of how God has blessed* you this year.

Second ... make a **list of the goals** you have for the next six months.

Third ... list the <u>*top three hindrances*</u> that you faced in the **first six months of this year**.

Fourth ... devise a *scriptural and practical strategy* to <u>overcome every hindrance, obstacle and roadblock</u>.

Fifth ... determine **who you need to involve** in the process.

Sixth ... create a **timeline to achieve every goal**.

14

Seventh … *monitor your progress* and think Rich Thoughts.

The Lord gave me *Seven Things God Hates* … and I typed them out … then I thought … that's great … I'll come back and write chapter two. I moved on to something else and then I came back a little less than an hour ago … and it was very clear to me **the Lord did not want me teaching seven things God hates**.

He wanted me to teach <u>*Seven Things You Should Do Today*</u> and I said Lord … you know … I just need to *give this more thought*.

Well … it didn't take long for me to get the message I was to do this today. So … you can know this teaching today is *directly for you from the throne room of God*.

It is to **provoke your thinking to move you outside your comfort zone**. It is for you to <u>personally reflect on this day to make a conscious and conscientious decision to plan the next six months of this year</u> … notice … we don't call it the last six months.

We call it the <u>*next six months*</u>. So here are **the next seven things the Lord gave me** … and I think **these are the ones that we really need to focus on**.

No. 1 … what is the one thing you are **most proud of that happened during the first six months** of this year?

It may come to your mind … immediately. You may have to think about it … and truthfully there may be many things that come to your mind … but just name one.

What is the one thing that you're most proud of that happened during the first six months of this year?

Once you identify it … *write it down*. Don't think about it … or meditate on it … just write it down … and once you do **praise God for it**.

Not only praise God for it, but tell *others about how good God's been to you*.

See, praising God is not just something we do *on Sunday morning* … or when *something pops in our head as a reflex* to what's going on around us. We say, "Well, praise God."

**Praising Him should be on a regular basis.**

Psalm 35:28 tells us:

*"And my tongue shall speak of thy righteousness and of thy praise all the day long."*

God will give us everything He's promised in His Word … because of that … **you and I can praise him and glorify him**.

Ephesians 1:14 in the New Living Translation tells us:

*"Who is the guarantee of our inheritance until we acquire possession of it, to the praise of his glory."*

**The Spirit is God's guarantee that He will give us the inheritance that He promised** … and He has purchased us *to be His own people* … He did this so we would *praise and glorify His name*.

I just can't stop praising his name … **Jesus** … **hallelujah**.

No. 2 … what is the greatest **miracle blessing that you experienced** in the first six months of this year? It could be the same as No. 1, but *I think there is a difference*.

For me it would be different … and truthfully my difficulty here is picking just one. There have been so many. **Don't allow the enemy to create negativity over some of the things you've had to go through during the first six months of this year.**

*Focus on praising Jesus for his blessings.*

Well … Brother Harold … no, there's no well, Brother Harold. You praise Him … *Praise Him that He woke you up this morning*. He clothed you in the mind of Christ.

**Praise Him that you have air to breathe … food to eat. Praise Him for it. Praise Him for it.**

What is the **greatest miracle blessing you've experienced** ... write it out.

No. 3 ... what is your No. 1 goal for the next six months ... and the reality is ... I have to ask you this. Did you have goals set at the beginning of the year ... or did you go through the first six months of the year *just reacting to what was happening around you instead of having a plan to make things happen*?

See, if we don't have goals ... then we allow someone else to have goals for us ... and **a goal is simply a vision of how it is before it is.**

**You need to have a goal ... a vision of how it's going to be ... because of the things God will instruct and allow you to accomplish.** You need to have those goals ... and if you didn't make goals for the first six months of this year, it's okay.

God wants to do a new thing for you starting right now. What's your one goal for the next six months, in the six major areas of your life?

It doesn't even have to be in each of those areas, *though I would recommend you do that.*

Spiritual ... family ... financial ... physical ... mental ... social ... what's your No. 1 goal? What's your No. 1 spiritual goal? What's your No. 1 family goal? What's your No. 1 financial or business goal?

**What is it?** What is it that you feel led to accomplish?

No. 4 … where's one area where you can create *more time for personal creativity and spiritual direction?*

Sometimes it just means that you need to stop doing what you're doing … to do something else … and yes, I can tell you from personal example … just because you're doing something and it's good … *doesn't mean God wants you to keep on doing it.*

I started doing half hour TV show six days a week on February 6, 2009. It was broadcast live around the world through streamingfaith.com, but a few days after Christmas that year … God showed me that *it took probably three hours of my time* between writing and recording every day for each program … and he directed me and showed me that if I stopped doing a live broadcast on Sunday … it would save me three hours a week or 156 hours a year … **roughly four work weeks** … and *that was time I could redirect somewhere else.*

**Is there something you can do to create more time for personal creativity and spirit, spiritual direction?** For some, it may be less time on television, less time on Facebook or social media or surfing the Internet … or *reading news about other people instead of creating the news yourself.*

No. 5 … what *habit would you most like to strengthen* during the next six months?

I'm asking these questions because *these are questions God wants you to answer today.*

We're talking about seven things you can do today to change your destiny ... so **don't get distracted**. Stay with me. I had a clear direction to do this ... and I know it's for **every person reading this book**. It is to *provoke your thinking outside your comfort zone.*

Back to No. 5 ... what's the one habit you'd most like to strengthen during the next six months and *what are you gonna do to do it?*

Is it exercise? If it is, **start**. If it's to alter your eating habits and lifestyle ... do it.

If it's to get your finances in order, **make it happen**. If it's to spend more time with your family ... <u>do it</u>. Don't talk about it ... **do it**.

No. 6 ... what's the one habit you'd like to get rid of immediately? There's some *bad habits we have that we need to get rid of* ... there's some *new habits we need to create.*

I need to give you No. 7 ... I need to give you a final thought.

What would it take to *keep you motivated* during the next six months? Identify what it will take to keep you *moving forward toward your goals* ... from where you are now ... **<u>to where you want to be</u>**.

Identify and do it.

Here's another question ... I've heard people say for

years … what would you do tomorrow if you couldn't fail?

Come on … tomorrow never comes.

**That's the naysayer's attitude.** I want to know what you would <u>do today because you could not fail</u>.

Job 42:2 in the Amplified Bible says:

> *"I know that you can do all things and that no thought or purpose of yours can be restrained nor thwarted."*

The Message Bible translation of Job 42:2 says:

> *"I'm convinced you can do anything and everything and nothing and no one can upset your plans."*

Every person hearing my voice is *empowered by the greatest force of the universe to achieve what others may think impossible*, **but it's not impossible for you.**

Luke 1:37 in the Amplified Bible says:

> *"For God, nothing is ever impossible and no word from God shall be without power or impossible of fulfillment."*

<u>**This is your day.**</u> There are certain things … that you can do today <u>to start turning your life around</u>.

This is your turn-around day. It is as clearly … as the *sun is shining outside my window* … as I'm looking out of it.

God directed me to do this message to provoke your thinking … that this is the day that you seize.

Carpe Diem. **Seize the Day.**

Answer these seven questions. *Provoke your thinking.* Create a place to talk to God … and **He'll help you find your way to better and better things**.

You may need to read this again, but I am telling you from the bottom of my heart … as much as I love you … and *I do love the people who make the effort to pick up this book* and read it every day.

*This is a word … **for you from God**.*

Father, I thank you for the unction of the Holy Ghost. *I thank you for the direction.* And Father … I just pray that the words I wrote were ordained of you. If not, bring correction and clarity where needed … and Father … help every person who reads my words today to **take charge of their destiny** to recognize that they are empowered to a "T" … and that what others may think impossible … *is possible in Your name.* Hallelujah and amen.

Happy trails … and **keep thinking Rich Thoughts**.

# Day 3

# 8 Things About Every Good Thing

What does it take to experience every good thing we have in Christ?

What is required for us to have a total understanding of *every* single *promise* we have in Christ?

The simple answer is found in Philemon 1:6 (New International Version) which says:

> *"I pray that you may be active in sharing your faith, so that you will have a full understanding of every good thing we have in Christ."*

Personalize it.

> *"I pray that <<Name>> may be active in sharing <<his/her>> faith, so that <<Name>> will have a full understanding of every good thing <<he/she>> has in Christ."*

**As we are actively sharing our faith, *we will gain a deeper, more complete revelation* of every good**

**thing that He has planned for us.**

Now I've got to be honest with you … *I really like, love and embrace the promise* that I can have every good thing I have in Christ.

How is He going to give us every good thing? *How will He provide for the manifestation of every good thing?* Are you ready for this?

Philippians 4:19 says:

> *"But my God shall supply all your need according to his riches in glory by Christ Jesus."*

I have discovered eight things about every good thing.

**1.      We're to rejoice and praise Him** *as He provides every good thing to us.*

Deuteronomy 26:11 says:

> *"And thou shalt rejoice in every good thing which the LORD thy God hath given unto thee, and unto thine house, thou, and the Levite, and the stranger that is among you."*

The New Living Translation of Deuteronomy 26:11 says:

> *"Afterward you may go and celebrate because of*

*all the good things the Lord your God has given to you and your household. Remember to include the Levites and the foreigners living among you in the celebration."*

*We're to celebrate every gift … every blessing … even the smallest things …* **WAIT, I take that back** *… God never does anything small for us … everything He does is big and meaningful and life changing.*

*WAIT again.* I sense someone just thought … "Maybe you, Brother Harold, but not me. *God hasn't done anything big or meaningful for me."*

Whoever you are, *I want you to stop right now and realize what a huge blessing it is that God gives you air to breathe every day.*

Have you stopped to think about all those who labor to breathe? They would gladly trade places with you right now *and that is only the beginning of your blessings. We all need to stop and be grateful for the many things we take for granted.*

We're also to celebrate not just what He's done for and provided to us but *every member of our household as well.*

**2.    We must recognize where every good thing that we enjoy and possess comes from.**

Psalm 16:2 in the New Living Translation says:

*"I said to the Lord, 'You are my Master! Every good thing I have comes from you.'"*

Everything on planet earth belongs to Him. *We own nothing ... but we get to manage everything!*

Notice the scripture says that every "good" thing comes from Him. **The Bible qualifies the things we receive from God.**

Sickness is not good ... God will never give you something that's not good.

Debt is not good ... God will never give you something that's not good.

Poverty and lack are not good ... God will never give you something that's not good.

**Your Heavenly Father gives you good gifts, *not bad, harmful or evil ones.***

Matthew 7:11 in the Amplified Bible says:

*"If you then, evil as you are, know how to give good and advantageous gifts to your children, how much more will your Father Who is in heaven [perfect as He is] give good and advantageous things to those who keep on asking Him!"*

## 3. We will be empowered in every good thing we do.

2 Thessalonians 2:16-17 in the New Living Translation says:

*"Now may our Lord Jesus Christ himself and God our Father, who loved us and by his grace gave us eternal comfort and a wonderful hope, comfort you and strengthen you in every good thing you do and say."*

When you're in the midst of a battle ... *you need the assurance that someone has your back. Someone who can give you peace and strength in the heat of every conflict.*

## 4. We will be given every good thing that gives Him pleasure.

Hebrews 13:21 in the New Living Translation says:

*"May he equip you with all you need for doing his will. May he produce in you, through the power of Jesus Christ, every good thing that is pleasing to him. All glory to him forever and ever! Amen."*

*He will only give us things that give Him pleasure.*

Psalm 35:27 says:

*"Let them shout for joy, and be glad, that favour*

*my righteous cause: yea, let them say continually, Let the LORD be magnified, which hath pleasure in the prosperity of his servant."*

What gives Him pleasure in every good thing … your prosperity.

**5.    We're to bless and honor those who bless us through the teaching of the Word.**

Galatians 6:6 in the Contemporary English Version says:

*"Share every good thing you have with anyone who teaches you what God has said."*

The Amplified Bible translation of Galatians 6:6 gives it a slightly different perspective.

*"Let him who receives instruction in the Word [of God] share all good things with his teacher [contributing to his support]."*

Yes, every good thing includes more than a pat on the back *and a "Great job … preacher"* … it includes financial seeds … *money is a part of every good thing.*

**6.    We're to produce the fruit of our salvation in every good thing we do.**

Colossians 1:10 in the New International Reader's Version says:

*"We pray that you will lead a life that is worthy of the Lord. We pray that you will please him in every way. So we want you to bear fruit in every good thing you do. We want you to grow to know God better."*

**7.    We have at our fingertips the master key to doing every good thing He wants us to do.**

Hebrews 13:20 in the New Century Version says:

*"I pray that the God of peace will give you every good thing you need so you can do what he wants."*

**Personalize this verse as you read it again.**

*"I pray that the God of peace will give <<Name>> every good thing <<he/she>> needs so <<Name>> can do what he wants."*

***You may wonder how we can know what good things He wants us to do.***

The answer which should be so obvious to every believer is found in 2 Timothy 3:17 in the New International Reader's Version which says:

*"By using Scripture, a man of God can be completely prepared to do every good thing."*

Do you remember the old Yellow Pages ad … "Let

your fingers do the walking." Well, that's so true when it comes to the scriptures.

*Every solution to every problem and possibility is right at our fingertips. And the computer makes it so much easier with topical word searches.*

Read your Bible ... do what it says.

8. **We must never ever forget that every good thing comes from Him and that's never going to change.**

James 1:17 in the New American Standard Version says:

*"Every good thing given and every perfect gift is from above, coming down from the Father of lights, with whom there is no variation or shifting shadow."*

Hebrews 13:8 says:

*"Jesus Christ the same yesterday, and today, and forever."*

Your Heavenly Father wanted you to have every good thing in Biblical times *and He still wants you to have the same thing today.*

*God hasn't changed His mind and the good news is*

*... **He never will.***

# Day 4

# 15 Thought Provoking Facts About July 4th

July 4th is not just another holiday.

It's much more than a trip to the beach, lake or pool. It's much more than a picnic in the park or backyard. This holiday is more than oohing and awing at fireworks displays.

July 4th is about freedom and liberty won and maintained through great personal sacrifice, commitment and faith.

Our independence was won by those who were willing to pay the ultimate price to that you and I could enjoy a holiday such as this.

I feel led to share with you 15 interesting, inspiring and thought-provoking facts about our July 4th, our freedom ... and the financial independence some have yet to achieve.

**1.    Psalm 33:12 says:**

*"Blessed is the nation whose God is the LORD; and the people whom he hath chosen for his*

*own inheritance."*

**2.    Patrick Henry said:**

*"It cannot be emphasized too strongly or too often that this great nation was founded, not by religionists, but by Christians, not on religions, but on the gospel of Jesus Christ!"*

**3.    George Washington said:**

*"It is impossible to rightly govern the world without God and the Bible."*

The following is a great story about General Washington's faith in God.

During the dark days of the American Revolution, when the Continental Army had experienced several setbacks, a farmer who lived near the battlefield approached Washington's camp unheard.

Suddenly his ears caught an earnest voice raised in agonizing prayer. On coming nearer he saw it was the great General, down on his knees in the snow, his cheeks wet with tears. He was asking God for assistance and guidance.

The farmer crept away and returned home. He said to his family, "It's going to be all right. We are going to win!"

"What makes you think so?" his wife asked.

"Well," said the farmer, "I heard General Washington praying out in the woods today—such fervent prayer I have never heard. And God will surely hear and answer that kind of praying."

And the farmer was right! It happened. *Fervent faith in God brings victory.*

## 4.  John Wayne said:

*"Sure I wave the American flag. Do you know a better flag to wave? Sure I love my country with all her faults. I'm not ashamed of that, never have been, never will be."*

## 5.  2 Chronicles 7:14 says:

*"If my people, who are called by my name, will humble themselves and pray and seek my face and turn from their wicked ways, then will I hear from heaven and will forgive their sin and will heal their land."*

## 6.  General Omar Bradley said:

*"America today is running on the momentum of a godly ancestry, and when that momentum runs down, God help America."*

## 7.  Proverbs 14:34 says:

*"Righteousness exalts a nation, but sin is a reproach to any people."*

## 8. Separation of Church and State has become confused over the years.

*My County, 'Tis of Thee* was written by a Baptist minister, Samuel Francis Smith.

*The Pledge of Allegiance* was written in 1892 by a Baptist minister, Francis Bellamy.

The words "In God We Trust" are traced to the efforts of Rev. W.R. Watkinson.

Twenty-nine of the fifty-six Signers of the Declaration of Independence had a seminary degree.

## 9. President John Quincy Adams said:

*"I speak as a man of the world to men of the world; and I say to you, Search the Scriptures! The Bible is the book of all others, to be read at all ages, and in all conditions of human life; not to be read once or twice or thrice through, and then laid aside, but to be read in small portions of one or two chapters every day, and never to be intermitted, unless by some overruling necessity."*

## 10. No King but Jesus!

The Colonists grew in their resilience and confidence in God, to the point where one Crown-appointed Governor wrote of the condition to the Board of Trade back in England: "If you ask an American who is his master? He will tell you he has none, nor any governor but Jesus Christ."

The Committees of Correspondence soon began sounding the cry across the Colonies: "No King but King Jesus!"

## 11.  General Douglas MacArthur

*"History fails to record a single precedent in which nations subject to moral decay have not passed into political and economic decline. There has been either a spiritual awakening to overcome the moral lapse, or a progressive deterioration leading to ultimate national disaster."*

## 12.  Abraham Lincoln

In June of 1863, just weeks before the battle of Gettysburg, a college president asked Abraham Lincoln if he thought the country would survive. President Lincoln replied:

*"I do not doubt that our country will finally come through safe and undivided. But do not misunderstand me ... I do not rely on the patriotism of our people ... the bravery and devotion of the boys in blue ... (or) the loyalty and skill of our generals ... But the God of our Fathers, Who raised up this country to be the refuge and asylum of the oppressed and the downtrodden of all nations will not let it perish now. I may not live to see it ... I do not expect to see it, but God will*

*bring us through safe."*

## 13. "Under God" and the Pledge of Allegiance

The words "under God" were taken from Abraham Lincoln's famous Gettysburg Address, "… that this nation, under God, shall have a new birth …" and were added to the Pledge of Allegiance on June 14, 1954.

*"I pledge allegiance to the flag of the United States of America, and to the Republic for which it stands, one nation under God, indivisible, with liberty and justice for all."*

## 14. Only in America (a humorous look at ourselves)

1. *Only in America can a pizza get to your house faster than an ambulance.*
2. *Only in America are there handicap parking places in front of a skating rink.*
3. *Only in America do drugstores make the sick walk all the way to the back of the store to get their prescriptions, while healthy people can buy cigarettes at the front.*
4. *Only in America do people order double cheeseburgers, large fries and a DIET coke.*
5. *Only in America do we leave cars worth thousands of dollars in the driveway and put our junk in the garage. Hello.*
6. *Only in America do we use answering machines to screen calls and have call-waiting so we won't miss a call from someone we didn't*

*want to talk to in the first place.*
7. *Only in America do we sell hot dogs in packages of ten and* buns in packages of eight.

## 15. Happy Birthday, America. I love you with a never-ending, ever-growing passion.

On July 4th, we celebrate our nation's independence ... *our freedom* **yet millions are not free ... financially speaking**.

If you spend more time worrying about the lack of money than you do making it, *then you're not free*. If you have to worry about which bill to pay or not pay, whether to give or not to give, then *you are definitely not free*. If you don't have money set aside for a proper retirement income, *you're not free*.

**Declaration of Financial Independence**

*Recognizing that I will never truly be free until I'm financially free, I declare my financial independence from debt and lack*.

As a born-again, Child of the Most High God, I do hereby:

1. Declare from this day forward ... I will be a faithful steward of ... everything that God entrusts to my care.

2. Declare I will see myself as God sees me ... filled with ... unlimited potential and possibilities.

3. Declare I'm getting out of debt rapidly … I will no longer be a slave to the moneylenders (Proverbs 22:7 CEV).

4. Declare I will create an open heaven with my tithes and … offerings.

5. Declare I will start speaking words that promote debt freedom and financial independence (Romans 4:17).

6. Declare I will create a plan to get out of debt and into financial freedom.

7. Declare I will study to show myself approved and with God's help achieve what He wants for me (I Kings 1:17; 2 Kings 4; Romans 13:8).

8. Declare that because God is no respecter of persons (Acts 10:34) I will never again use excuses to justify anything but excellence and effective stewardship.

When you agree to this prayer … *we will be praying for you along with our friends and partners from around the world.* We will pray for you to summon the courage to fight for your freedom. Stick with it like our forefathers did … *as though your life depends upon it* … because it does.

And keep thinking Rich Thoughts.

**Day 5**

# 7 Things About Your Past to Assure Your Future

I'm going to say eighteen words … if you get nothing else from this teaching but these eighteen words … *your life will never be the same.*

When I say "get it" … I mean … "get it" … *deep down inside* … so that no circumstance or problem *can ever cause you to forget this powerful truth* … even in the heat of battle.

Are you ready? I want you to say it out loud with me. Ready?

**"God will never do a new thing in my life … as long as I'm holding onto the past."**

Need a confirming scripture? 2 Corinthians 5:17 says:

*"Therefore if any man be in Christ, he is a new creature: old things are passed away; behold, all things are become new."*

You must get rid of the old … to ever embrace the new.

Let's look at 7 things about your past to assure you a prosperous future.

## 1.    You've Got a Past

Where you are today ... *is a result of the choices you made yesterday.* Where you will be tomorrow *will be the result of the choices you make today.*

Now I fully realize that some of you are dealing with situations today *because of choices dysfunctional family members made for you yesterday.*

However, what happened to you in the past *doesn't give you an excuse for your behavior in the future.*

If you're drawing a breath on planet earth ... *I'm confident there some things in your past that you're not particularly proud of* ... but it's now history.

Your past ... the old thing that's passing away ... *was never designed to enslave you to where you are ... doing what you've been doing. The night of your past is turning to day.*

Romans 13:12 in the Contemporary English Version says:

*"Night is almost over, and day will soon appear. We must stop behaving as people do in the dark and be ready to live in the light."*

It's time for you to live in the light of His Word.

## 2.    You Can't Change the Past

What's done is done ... but you can change the con-sequences of your future by decisions you make to-day.

Oscar Wilde, the great playwright, said:

**"No man is rich enough to buy back his past."**

*There's no need to change your past ... when it's been forgiven. God is ready to do a new thing in your life.*

Isaiah 43:18-19 in the Amplified Bible says:

*"Do not [earnestly] remember the former things; neither consider the things of old. Behold, I am doing a new thing! Now it springs forth; do you not perceive and know it and will you not give heed to it? I will even make a way in the wilder-ness and rivers in the desert."*

If you've messed up ... fess up ... get up and move on.

I'm going to say this one more time ... not only are you unable to change the past ... you don't need to ... because you've been forgiven.

## 3.    You Can't Blame the Past

There is never a winner when you play the blame game ... *even if your behavior makes you the Most Valuable Player of the game.*

If you'd only done this ... yes, *but if you'd only done that.*

Do you know who wins in such a conversation? *If you say, "nobody" ... you'd be wrong.* The enemy of your soul ... WINS.

Hosea 4:4 in the New Living Translation says:

> *"Don't point your finger at someone else and try to pass the blame! My complaint, you priests, is with you."*

## 4. You Don't Need to Be Controlled by Your Past

Let's establish another absolute fact.

God will never remind you of your past. He can't ... He's forgotten it.

Here are two confirming scriptures.

First, Hebrews 8:12 in the New Living Translation says:

> *"And I will forgive their wickedness, and I will never again remember their sins."*

Second, Jeremiah 31:34 in the Contemporary English Version says:

> *"No longer will they have to teach one another to obey me. I, the LORD, promise that all of them will obey me, ordinary people and rulers alike. I will forgive their sins and <u>forget the evil things</u> they have done."*

At this moment ... you should be asking yourself the obvious question.

*If God is not reminding me of my past ... then who is?*

The answer is painfully obvious ... the accuser of the brethren ... the devil of debt, lack and everything else evil and/or bad.

Job 2:1 in the New Living Translation says:

> *"One day the members of the heavenly court came again to present themselves before the LORD, and the Accuser, Satan, came with them."*

Why would you ever allow something that's been forgiven and forgotten to distract you from your future successes?

**5. You Must Take Responsibility for Your Past**

If you continue to blame everyone else for your mistakes ... *you'll never become what God intended you to be.*

I have far greater respect for someone who takes responsibility for their mistakes than someone who tries to cover them up or shift the blame to someone else.

Proverbs 28:13 in The Living Bible offers good advice we need to listen to:

> *"A man who refuses to admit his mistakes can never be successful. But if he confesses and forsakes them, he gets another chance."*

The best approach, in fact, the scriptural approach is just to fess up when we make a mistake.

By confessing your sins … you're heading in the right direction … His.

Proverbs 24:15-16 in the Message Bible says:

> *"Don't interfere with good people's lives; don't try to get the best of them. No matter how many times you trip them up, God-loyal people don't stay down long; Soon they're up on their feet, while the wicked end up flat on their faces."*

Joe Louis, the famous Heavyweight Champion of the world, once said:

> *"If life knocks you down … try to land on your back … because if you can look up … you can get up."*

## 6.    You Must Change

You will be judged by your reputation of the past until you do something to change your reputation of the future.

If you're willing to change ... things will change. If you're not ... they won't.

Don't worry about changing other people ... change yourself and you'll be amazed at how quickly they change.

The only way to effectively change your circumstances is for you to personally change how you look at them.

TODAY ... do the things necessary to change your future into the reality you desire.

President John F. Kennedy said:

**"Change is the law of life. And those who look only to the past are certain to miss the future."**

God has a bright future planned for you ... don't miss it by living in the past and refusing to change for the future.

## 7.    You Must Not Let Your Past Define You

Never allow your past to determine your future.

Patrick Henry, the American patriot, said:

**"I like dreams of the future better than the history of the past."**

You can't change your past … but you can re-direct your future.

Ralph Waldo Emerson, the great American poet, said:

**"With the past, I have nothing to do; nor with the future. I live now."**

Proverbs 24:14 in the New Living Translation says:

*"In the same way, wisdom is sweet to your soul. If you find it, you will have a bright future, and your hopes will not be cut short."*

Denis Waitley, the author and motivational speaker, said:

**"Losers live in the past. Winners learn from the past and enjoy working in the present toward the future."**

Habakkuk 2:3 in the New Living Translation says:

*"This vision is for a future time. It describes the end, and it will be fulfilled. If it seems slow in coming, wait patiently, for it will surely take place. It will not be delayed."*

One more thing … don't let people you've known in

the past … try to keep you where you were before.

You're past is forgiven and forgotten … you're ready for a new thing and you're never looking back.

**Day 6**

# 7 Reasons You Will Be Rewarded

If you need encouragement in the battle … strength to carry on … wisdom to understand what's happening to you or around you … insight on your future success … then this teaching is for you.

Isaiah 45:19 in the Amplified Bible offers 7 amazing promises.

> *"I have not spoken in secret (1), in a corner of the land of darkness; I did not call the descendants of Jacob [to a fruitless service] (2), saying, Seek Me for nothing (3) [but I promised them a just reward] (4). I, the Lord, speak righteousness (the truth—trustworthy (5), straightforward correspondence between deeds and words) (6); I declare things that are right. (7)"*

I'm convinced beyond any doubt … *God wants you to see*, understand and *expect the manifestation of these seven promises in your life NOW … RIGHT NOW!*

**First, God makes no secret about the kind of life**

**He wants us to have.**

_The enemy of our success will try to deceive us into_
_believing where we are and what we have ... is all_
_there will ever be_. It's a lie because he's a liar.

3 John 2 says:

> *"Beloved, I wish above all things that <<Your*
> *name>> mayest prosper and be in health, even*
> *as your soul prospereth."*

God's plan is very clear. However, you determine your
steps by the decisions you make and the actions you
take.

**Second, God called us to produce fruit with our**
**lives.**

As we move out of our comfort zone ... *becoming*
*productive for the kingdom* ... God will make us prosperous in all our hands find to do.

Deuteronomy 30:9 says:

> *"And the Lord your God will make you abundant-*
> *ly prosperous in every work of your hand, in the*
> *fruit of your body, of your cattle, of your land, for*
> *good; for the Lord will again delight in prospering*
> *you, as He took delight in your fathers."*

I just have to tell you ... *it makes me want to shout,*
*"Hallelujah! Thank You Jesus,"* when I read how the

*Lord delights in prospering me.*

Not just anybody, but He wants to prosper me. He wants me to be "abundantly prosperous."

We must be productive … in *what we do* … must be making a difference … *not only in our lives* … but in the lives of those we come in contact with.

John 15:16 says:

> *"Ye have not chosen me, but I have chosen you, and ordained you, that ye should go and bring forth fruit, and that your fruit should remain: that whatsoever ye shall ask of the Father in my name, he may give it you."*

**When you're productive in the Kingdom … God will give you whatever you ask of Him.**

What an offer … we'd have to be a hamburger short of a happy meal to *not take advantage of this life-changing offer.*

**Third, when we seek Him things happen!**

About a year and a half ago, God gave me seven words that … *when applied* … will change your life forever. READ YOUR BIBLE … DO WHAT IT SAYS.

Jeremiah 29:12-14 in the Message Bible says:

> *"Then you will call upon Me, and you will come*

*and pray to Me, and I will hear and heed you. Then you will seek Me, inquire for, and require Me [as a vital necessity] and find Me when you search for Me with all your heart. I will be found by you, says the Lord, and I will release you from captivity ..."*

Too often when we face adversity ... *we talk to ... share our problems with people who can only listen* ... maybe, *even give good advice* ... but, *otherwise do nothing to solve our problem* or *bring any sort of relief in the middle of the adversity.*

We talk to the banker when we can't make our payments ... asking him to fix or delay our problems ... when God can supernaturally eliminate our debts.

We talk to the counselor about our problems in our marriage ... *when God can heal the broken-hearted* and *restore what the enemy has tried to tear asunder.*

Matthew 21:22 in the Amplified Bible says:

*"And whatever you ask for in prayer, having faith and [really] believing, you will receive."*

**Fourth, we've got a reward coming.**

At various times in your life ... you may have been rewarded ... by a parent for good behavior ... by a teacher for making good grades ... a coach for a great game ... by an employer for doing a job well. *But you can't even begin to imagine* ... the kind of rewards coming for your obedience to His direction. ***God owes NO ONE ... you will receive your reward.***

Hebrews 11:6 says:

> *"But without faith it is impossible to please him: for he that cometh to God must believe that he is, and that he is a rewarder of them that diligently seek him."*

According to Strong's Concordance the Greek word for rewarder is misthapodotēs (G3406) and it means:

**"one who pays wages, a rewarder."**

**He is one who pays wages to them that diligently seek him.**

Are you getting this?

Jeremiah 17:10 in the New Living Translation says:

> *"But I, the Lord, search all hearts and examine secret motives. I give all people their due rewards, according to what their actions deserve."*

What are your due rewards for diligently seeking him? You're going to get paid for it.

Hallelujah!!

**Fifth, walk in righteousness.**

There is a powerful life-changing truth found in 1 Peter 2:24 which says:

*"Who his own self bare our sins in his own body on the tree, that we, being dead to sins, should live unto righteousness: by whose stripes ye were healed."*

The key to this verse and life is these four words: *"should live unto righteousness."*

I looked up the word righteousness in the Strong's Concordance and found that it's the Greek word dikaiosynē (G1343) which means:

**"in a broad sense: state of him who is as he ought to be, righteousness, the condition acceptable to God: integrity, virtue, purity of life, rightness, correctness of thinking feeling, and acting."**

That's when I saw it ... ***righteousness* is the "state of him who is as he ought to be."**

How "ought" we to be?

We ought to ***be dead to sin*** ... so **we can have "correctness of thinking, feeling and acting."**

<u>Sin is what keeps us</u> **from thinking right ... feeling right ... acting right ... living right.**

The <u>purpose of sin is to separate us from the love</u>

God has for us ... that's why we must walk in right-eousness ... if we want to receive His reward.

**Sixth, our faithfulness to God produces great rewards.**

God is not looking for below average or even average stewards. He's looking for believers who understand and practice faithfulness, integrity and excellence.

Matthew 25:2 in the New Living Translation says:

*"Now, a person who is put in charge as a manager must be faithful."*

No doubt about it ... God is looking for faithfulness in His stewards. It's His criteria for being an effective steward.

Matthew 25:14-15 says:

*"For the kingdom of heaven is as a man travelling into a far country, who called his own servants, and delivered unto them his goods. And unto one he gave five talents, to another two, and to another one; to every man according to his several ability; and straightway took his journey."*

What you have at the moment is what God thinks you can handle ... but if you prove yourself faithful ... you were be given more and more.

**Seventh, God is going to make all things right!**

Isaiah 61:7 in the New Living Translation says:

*"Instead of shame and dishonor, you will enjoy a double share of honor. You will possess a double portion of prosperity in your land, and everlasting joy will be yours."*

Child of God, you're not just going to receive the land … your inheritance … you're going to get a double portion of prosperity.

When you follow the principles of Isaiah 45:19 … not only will you be rewarded, blessed and prospered … God is going to turn your sorrow into joy.

Now that's what I call a great reward … a double dose of prosperity and the joy that comes with it.

# Day 7

## 7 Reasons You Need S.A.L.T.

Philippians 2:3 in the Amplified Bible says:

> *"Do nothing from factional motives [through contentiousness, strife, selfishness, or for unworthy ends] or prompted by conceit and empty arrogance. Instead, in the true spirit of humility (lowliness of mind) let each regard the others as better than and superior to himself [thinking more highly of one another than you do of yourselves]."*

In reading this verse we learn there are seven things we're told not to do.

## 1.  Do nothing from factional motives.

According to dictionary.com the word "factional" means:

**"self-interested."**

Sadly, many people are only interested in whether or

not something benefits them.

Matthew 20:26 in the Contemporary English Version says:

*But don't act like them. If you want to be great, you must be the servant of all the others."*

When a verse is repeated twice in scripture you can know *that it must be important to God* ... and if it's important to Him ... *it had better be important to us.*

Mark 10:43 in the Contemporary English Version says:

*"But don't act like them. If you want to be great, you must be the servant of all the others."*

The scriptures point out that greatness is personified in the service of others.

Matthew 23:11 says:

*"But he that is greatest among you shall be your servant."*

If you want to be considered great in the Kingdom of God ... serve someone else ... when nobody is looking.

## 2.    Do nothing through contentiousness.

According to dictionary.com the word "contentiousness" as listed in Philippians 2:3 in the Amplified Bible is defined as:

**"tending to argument; quarrelsome."**

*Have you ever been around anyone who just likes to argue?*

Maybe a family, friend, co-worker or just someone you sit beside in a restaurant.

Certain people seem to relish arguing about everything with anybody.

It's easy to get drawn into discussions with contentious people … *however, I strongly recommend you avoid the temptation. You certainly don't want to act like or be known as that kind of person.*

I would, however, like to encourage you to follow the wisdom of a dear friend of this ministry … Pam from Valrico, Florida, once gave one of the most powerful and appropriate anagrams of SALT that I've ever heard.

S … Stop

A … Acting

L … Like

T … Them

The best way to **S**top **A**cting **L**ike **T**hem is not to allow yourselves to become argumentative even in self-defense. Instead, let God be your defender.

## 3.    **Do nothing through strife.**

James 3:16 says:

> *"For where envying and strife is, there is confusion and every evil work."*

I have a historical background in politics *and a unique understanding of how the system works … and what motivates and/or frustrates voters.*

One of the things I dislike intensely is when people interrupt and talk over other people without letting them express their opinion. *Even if I completely disagree with what you're saying …* I'm going to wait my turn to speak … *doing anything else is just plain rude and creates strife.*

I find it interesting that the Greek word for strife (eritheia G2052) is defined in Strong's Concordance as:

### "electioneering or intriguing for office, a desire to put one's self forward."

I'd say that's *an apt description* of the state of political dialogue in this country.

However, it becomes even more interesting when you

realize the Greek root word for strife (erethizō G2042) means:

**"to stir up, to provoke."**

When you provoke someone … you're causing trouble that will come back to haunt you.

### 4.    Do nothing selfish.

I can give you a great reason not to be selfish and it's confirmed with almost identical scriptures found in Matthew 16:24; Mark 8:34 and Luke 9:24, three of the Gospels.

Matthew 16:24 in the New Living Translation says:

> *"Then Jesus said to his disciples, 'If any of you wants to be my follower, you must turn from your selfish ways, take up your cross, and follow me.'"*

Bottom line … God does not want us to be selfish.

In fact, Philippians 2:4 in the Amplified Bible admonishes us to always be concerned about the interests of others. It says:

> *"Let each of you esteem and look upon and be concerned for not [merely] his own interests, but also each for the interests of others."*

**<u>Our thoughts and actions will either be dominated</u>**

**by our flesh which is selfish or our spirit which is selfless.** We choose.

## 5.    Do nothing for unworthy ends or reasons.

If something is not unworthy then it's worthy ... so clearly, *the scripture is telling us to do things that are worthy of our lineage, as a joint heir with Christ ... and our calling.*

Ephesians 4:1 in the Amplified Bible says:

> *"I THEREFORE, the prisoner for the Lord, appeal to and beg you to walk (lead a life) worthy of the [divine] calling to which you have been called [with behavior that is a credit to the summons to God's service."*

In the final analysis, you want to be declared worthy.

2 Thessalonians 1:11 in the Amplified Bible says:

> *"With this in view we constantly pray for you, that our God may deem and count you worthy of [your] calling and [His] every gracious purpose of goodness, and with power may complete in [your] every particular work of faith (faith which is that leaning of the whole human personality on God in absolute trust and confidence in His power, wisdom, and goodness."*

If you want to hang around with worthy people ... prove yourself to be worthy.

## 6.    Do nothing through conceit.

There is only one thing you need to know about being conceited and it's found in Proverbs 16:5 in the Contemporary English Version where it says:

*"The LORD doesn't like anyone who is conceited-- you can be sure they will be punished."*

Do you need more clarification on what the scripture means? Consider the words of Proverbs 16:5 in the Amplified Bible which says:

*"Everyone proud and arrogant in heart is disgusting, hateful, and exceedingly offensive to the Lord; be assured [I pledge it] they will not go unpunished."*

If you're conceited … it is *"… disgusting, hateful, and exceedingly offensive to the Lord …"*

## 7.    Do nothing through empty arrogance.

Here are seven things you need to know about being arrogant.

### 1. Arrogance will always be exposed.

1 Samuel 2:3 in the New Living Translation says:

*"Stop acting so proud and haughty! Don't speak with such arrogance! For the Lord is a God who*

*knows what you have done; he will judge your actions."*

## 2. Arrogant people always lie.

Psalm 59:12 in the New Living Translation says:

*"Because of the sins from their mouths and the words on their lips. Let them be trapped by their own arrogance because they speak curses and lies."*

## 3. Arrogance aborts wisdom from your life.

Proverbs 13:10 in the New Living Translation says:

*"Arrogance produces only quarreling, but those who take advice gain wisdom."*

## 4. Arrogance knows no boundaries.

Proverbs 21:24 in the New Living Translation says:

*"An arrogant, conceited person is called a mocker. His arrogance knows no limits."*

## 5. Arrogance at any level must be arrested.

2 Corinthians 10:5 in the New Living Translation says:

*"And all their intellectual arrogance that oppose the knowledge of God. We take every thought captive so that it is obedient to Christ."*

## 6. Arrogance hangs out with some pretty nasty folks.

Mark 7:22 in the New Living Translation says:

*"Greed, wickedness, cheating, shameless lust, envy, cursing, arrogance, and foolishness come from within a person."*

## 7. Wealth erodes an arrogant person's moral center.

Ezekiel 28:5 in the Contemporary English Version says:

*"You're a clever businessman and are extremely wealthy, but your wealth has led to arrogance!"*

I began this teaching with Philippians 2:1-4 and I want to close with that passage … this time from The Message Bible which says:

*"If you've gotten anything at all out of following Christ, if his love has made any difference in your life, if being in a community of the Spirit means anything to you, if you have a heart, if you care— then do me a favor:*

*"Agree with each other, love each other, be deep-spirited friends. Don't push your way to the front; don't sweet-talk your way to the top.*

*"Put yourself aside, and help others get ahead. Don't be obsessed with getting your own advantage. Forget yourselves long enough to lend a helping hand."*

It's time to **S**top **A**cting **L**ike **T**hem and begin acting **more like Him**.

**Day 8**

# 7 Ways to Hush Your Circumstances

Mark 4:29-30 in the Amplified Bible says:

> *"And He arose and rebuked the wind and said to the sea, Hush now! Be still (muzzled)! And the wind ceased (sank to rest as if exhausted by its beating) and there was [immediately] a great calm (a perfect peacefulness). He said to them, Why are you so timid and fearful? How is it that you have no faith (no firmly relying trust)?"*

The disciplines and Jesus were crossing the Sea of Galilee *when a storm began to rage*. The disciples were frightened, *fearful* and *faithless in the midst of what they perceived to be a deadly situation*.

Here are seven ways to hush your circumstances … or deal with the storms you're facing.

**1.    When trouble is headed your way … always do what Jesus did.**

When the storms of live rise up against you … be at peace.

When troubles come your way … *do you find yourself having sleepless nights … tossing and turning …* worrying about what may or may not happen?

Don't you think Jesus knew there was a storm forming … *about to churn into a dangerous situation?* We should follow His direction as found in the Contemporary English Version of Mark 4:38 which says:

> *"Jesus was in the back of the boat with his head on a pillow, and he was asleep."*

Matthew 6:34 in the Message Bible offers some great advice when it says:

> *"Give your entire attention to what God is doing right now, and don't get worked up about what may or may not happen tomorrow. God will help you deal with whatever hard things come up when the time comes."*

## 2. Always know He will never tell you to do anything dangerous *without a way of escape.*

Mark 4:35 in the Amplified Bible says:

> *"On that same day [when] evening had come, He said to them, Let us go over to the other side [of the lake]."*

Did you believe the Son of God knew what was going to happen … *before it ever happened?*

Acts 2:23 in the New Living Translation says:

> *"But God knew what would happen, and his pre-arranged plan was carried out when Jesus was betrayed. With the help of lawless Gentiles, you nailed him to a cross and killed him."*

If He knew He was going to be betrayed and crucified … *He most certainly knew about a storm in the Sea of Galilee.*

Since Jesus knew the storm was coming … *do you really think He would have put the disciples … those closest to Him … in a position to drown and die?* Of course, not!

In everything you face in life … no matter how great the temptation or seemingly insurmountable the problem may be … God always provides a way of escape.

1 Corinthians 10:13 says:

> *"There hath no temptation taken you but such as is common to man: but God is faithful, who will not suffer you to be tempted above that ye are able; but will with the temptation also make a way to escape, that ye may be able to bear it."*

## 3.    God is not moved by your circumstances … and neither should you be.

If you're doing what God has called you to do … *fulfilling His vision for your life … being obedient to His divine direction* … stuff is going to happen.

The enemy will do everything he can to render you ineffective *for and to* the Kingdom of God.

Isaiah 41:10 in the Message Bible says:

> *"Don't panic. I'm with you. There's no need to fear for I'm your God. I'll give you strength. I'll help you. I'll hold you steady, keep a firm grip on you."*

## 4.      When in the midst of the storms of life … call on Him and quote the Word.

When trouble comes … who you gonna call? *Not Ghostbusters* … but the Holy Ghost.

Psalm 86:5-7 says:

> *"In the day of my trouble I will call upon thee: for thou wilt answer me."*

If you need the peace of God in your life … *if you need deliverance from the storms of adversity* … heed the words of Jeremiah 29:12-14 in the Amplified Bible which says:

> *"Then you will call upon Me, and you will come and pray to Me, and I will hear and heed you. Then you will seek Me, inquire for, and require Me [as a vital necessity] and find Me when you search for Me with all your heart. I will be found*

*by you, says the Lord, and I will release you from captivity …"*

Now here's a revelation … *you can't quote what you don't know.*

Matthew 22:29 in the New Living Translation says:

*"Jesus replied, 'Your mistake is that you don't know the Scriptures, and you don't know the power of God.'"*

## 5.    When you rely on the Word … all your fears will leave.

The best reason not to be afraid … *is because the Word of God tells you not to.*

Isaiah 41:10 in the Contemporary English Version says:

*"Don't be afraid. I am with you. Don't tremble with fear. I am your God. I will make you strong, as I protect you with my arm and give you victories."*

Psalm 118:6 in the Message Bible says:

*"God's now at my side and I'm not afraid; who would dare lay a hand on me?"*

Deuteronomy 20:1 in the Message Bible says:

*"… In a few minutes you're going to do battle*

*with your enemies. Don't waver in resolve. Don't fear. Don't hesitate. Don't panic. God, your God, is right there with you, fighting with you against your enemies, fighting to win."*

Psalm 139:5 in the Message Bible says:

*"You know when I leave and when I get back; I'm never out of your sight. You know everything I'm going to say before I start the first sentence. I look behind me and you're there, then up ahead and you're there, too—your reassuring presence, coming and going. This is too much, too wonderful—I can't take it all in!"*

## 6. When facing adversity ... you need to tell your circumstances and those around you to "Hush."

Sometimes you may even have to tell your friends ... more properly known as acquaintances ... *to hush ... because at the first sign of adversity ...* they're gone faster than a snowman in 50-degree sunshine.

However, for those who either comment before bolting or hang around ... *never let the second voice distract you from what you know to be spiritual truth and your ability to allow God's power to work through you.*

Mark 4:39 in the Amplified Bible says:

*"And He arose and rebuked the wind and said to the sea, Hush now! Be still (muzzled)! And the*

*wind ceased (sank to rest as if exhausted by its beating) and there was [immediately] a great calm (a perfect peacefulness)."*

## 7.    Always be willing to learn in every situation.

Philippians 4:11 in the New Living Translation says:

*"I'm not saying this because I'm in any need. I've learned to be content in whatever situation I'm in."*

This scripture is most often misunderstood … it's not a scriptural admonition to settle for what you've got in life.

I've gone through some things in my life … and I've wanted to learn everything I could in those situations … so I would **never have to experience them again**.

Philippians 4:12 in the New Living Translation says:

*"I know how to live on almost nothing or with everything. I have learned the secret of living in every situation, whether it is with a full stomach or empty, with plenty or little."*

God clearly wants us to learn how to survive, over-come and be victorious in every adversity that we face.

I strongly suggest you meditate on Philippians 4:13 in the Message Bible which says:

*"Whatever I have, wherever I am, I can make it*

*through anything in the One who makes me who I am."*

The only way God can mold you into the person He wants you to be … is by your willingness to *learn from every situation you face*.

One final scripture in this teaching … 2 Corinthians 1:3-4 in the Message Bible says:

*"All praise to the God and Father of our Master, Jesus the Messiah! Father of all mercy! God of all healing counsel! He comes alongside us when we go through hard times, and before you know it, he brings us alongside someone else who is going through hard times so that we can be there for that person just as God was there for us."*

Your Heavenly Father is teaching you His way … *24 hours a day.*

**And sometimes you just need to learn how to say HUSH.**

**Day 9**

# 7 Things That Will Bring the House Down

Are you familiar with the expression *"bringing the house down"*?

Would you like to achieve that feat? If so, just don't do it … *the way Sampson did.*

Sorry, I couldn't resist the humor.

In looking at Samson's life we can clearly identify seven things that led to bringing the house down.

## 1.    Disobeying your father (or mother or both)

Samson's parents valued his covenant … *honored the God of their fathers* and knew right from wrong.

Judges 14:3 in the New Living Translation says:

> *"His father and mother objected. 'Isn't there even one woman in our tribe or among all the Israelites you could marry?' they asked. 'Why must you go to the pagan Philistines to find a wife?'"*

Samson's rationale for picking his bride wasn't based on her heart *or what was in her head.*

Judges 14:3 in the New Living Translation concludes by saying:

*"But Samson told his father, 'Get her for me! She looks good to me.'"*

*Samson's parents knew his decision would lead to trouble.*

Judges 14:4 says:

*"But his father and his mother knew not that it was of the LORD ..."*

As parents there is a point where you have to say "No." *I can tell you at times it's difficult to do so.* The earlier the boundaries are drawn ... will save you and your children from *headaches and heartaches* later on down the road.

It's also important to understand that **parents often do their very best ...** ***telling their children what's right and what's wrong*** **... only to have the children make the wrong choices**.

<u>If you've taught your children right from wrong and they choose wrongly ... don't let the enemy beat you up over it</u>. You did what was right. The decision to do wrong was your child's choice, not yours.

That's from Dr. J.E. Murdock, the founder and senior pastor of The Wisdom Center in Fort Worth, Texas.

## 2.    Pride

With an anointing like *Samson's* or anybody else for that matter … there must be humility *or spiritual and emotional pride will gain a foothold.*

I think it's fair to say that Samson had a bit of an ego.

Before you rush to condemn Samson for his ego … it's important to point out that a man without an ego isn't any good either … because he will never get anything done. However, **the measure of a man or for that matter … or a woman … is the extent to which his ego is sanctified**.

Earlier in Judges 14 Samson had slain a lion with his bare hands. *Some time later while traveling to his wedding Samson passed the carcass of the lion he had slain.* He noticed that a swarm of bees had made honey in the carcass (Judges 14:8-9).

Samson was obviously a bit cocky not only about his feat of strength *but his ability to put forth a riddle not one would understand or figure out.*

Proverbs 16:18 in the Message Bible says:

> *"First pride, then the crash—the bigger the ego, the harder the fall."*

**Oftentimes, people with an overly inflated ego will not accept responsibility for their own actions.** _When trouble comes_ ... _it's always somebody else's fault_.

Judges 15:4 in the New Living Translation says:

> _"Samson said, 'This time I cannot be blamed for everything I am going to do to you Philistines.'"_

A bruised ego ... is a tragic and often reckless thing.

### 3.    Sex

Judges 14:1 in the New Living Translation says:

> _"One day when Samson was in Timnah, (Tim naa) one of the Philistine women caught his eye."_

The woman caught Samson's eye because of how she looked ... her sex appeal.

Judges 14:3 in the New Living Translation concludes by saying:

> _"But Samson told his father, 'Get her for me! She looks good to me.'"_

Judges 16:1 in the New Living Translation says:

> _"One day Samson went to the Philistine town of Gaza and spent the night with a prostitute."_

It's clear that Samson was hanging out with the kind of women that his Momma had no doubt warned him about.

## 4.    Playing with temptation

*The quickest way into trouble is to compromise with sin.*

Samson obviously had an eye for beautiful women. *It didn't matter to him if they were saints or sinners …* as long as they appealed to his flesh.

He was continually traveling into enemy territory … going into the land of the Philistines looking for attractive women … *some of whom were prostitutes.*

Judges 16:1 in the New Living Translation says:

> *"One day Samson went to the Philistine town of Gaza and spent the night with a prostitute."*

**Never put yourself in an environment where evil is present *especially if the area of temptation is a weakness to you*.**

## 5.    Taking your gift for granted

In Judges 14:14-17 the men of Judah took Samson captive with his permission … bound him with two new ropes and turned him over the Philistines.

When the Philistines arrived to take Samson, the

scripture in Judges 14:14 says:

> *"The Spirit of the LORD came powerfully upon Samson ..."*

On that day over 1,000 Philistines were slain by Samson using the jawbone of a donkey as his weapon.

When the last Philistine died the scripture in Judges 14:16-17 in the New Living Translation says:

> *"Then Samson said, 'With the jawbone of a donkey, I've piled them in heaps! With the jawbone of a donkey, I've killed a thousand men!' When he finished his boasting, he threw away the jawbone ..."*

**Samson bragged about his abilities but not the One who gave him those abilities.**

Before we're too quick to condemn Samson ... there is a question each of us must answer.

**<u>Do we always credit the Holy Spirit for enabling, enlightening and empowering us to achieve the things we do in life</u>?**

**6.     Lying even if to an enemy**

Lying is wrong. <u>Lying is not a game played for sport ...</u> *<u>but rather a seed of deception</u>* <u>which will produce an undesired harvest</u>.

In Judges 16 we read where Delilah kept asking Samson the source of his strength and *three times he lied to her* … no doubt with a smile on his face.

Judges 16:15 in the Amplified Bible says:

> *"And she said to him, How can you say, I love you, when your heart is not with me? You have mocked me these three times and have not told me in what your great strength lies."*

If you live a life of lies … soon you will fall prey to your own deception.

## 7.    Minimizing God's instructions to you

When Samson finally yielded to Delilah's nagging treachery … he got more trouble than he could handle.

Judges 16:20 in the Amplified Bible says:

> *"She said, The Philistines are upon you, Samson! And he awoke out of his sleep and said, I will go out as I have time after time and shake myself free. For Samson did not know that the Lord had departed from him."*

When you minimize or ignore God's instructions … trouble is coming to your house.

The Philistines gouged out Samson's eyes and made fun of him. Finally, all their leaders and many of the people gathered in the Temple of Dagon to make sport of Samson.

You no doubt know the story … he asked a young boy near him to put his hands on the columns.

Judges 16:28 in the Amplified Bible says:

> *"Then Samson called to the Lord and said, O Lord God, [earnestly] remember me, I pray You, and strengthen me, I pray You, only this once, O God, and let me have one vengeance upon the Philistines for both my eyes."*

Samson grabbed both main pillars of the temple and pushed … bringing the house down.

Judges 16:30 in the Amplified Bible says:

> *"And Samson cried, Let me die with the Philistines! And he bowed himself mightily, and the house fell upon the princes and upon all the people that were in it. So the dead whom he slew at his death were more than they whom he slew in his life."*

*God wants your entire life to be productive …* **but you must obey His instructions**.

Disrespect for authority … yielding to temptation … pride … deception … minimizing or ignoring God's instructions *always leads to trouble* …

**Day 10**

# God Doesn't Want the Credit

In traveling the globe I've heard all sorts of things attributed to God. Things that truthfully … I know … *He wouldn't have anything to do with.*

How can I make such a bold statement**? If you know what a person says doesn't line up with the Word … then it's not God.** That part is easy.

I can't begin to tell you how many women have told me that God told them "so and so" was going to be their husband. *The only problem is that "so and so" is already married to someone else.*

They didn't want to change their minds even when I quoted Matthew 19:6:

> *"Wherefore they are no more twain, but one flesh. What therefore God hath joined together, let not man put asunder."*

Seriously, after quoting that scripture, on more than one occasion I've been told, "Yes, I know that verse, but I also know what God told me."

That's not just ignorance gone to seed ... *it's spiritual stupidity* and it's very dangerous.

A couple once approached me whose finances were in complete disarray ... the man was nearly blind which restricted his self-employed opportunities as an accountant. His work was such *that if he didn't work,* they had no income. His wife didn't have an outside job.

I remember them telling me with great excitement how God had made it possible for them to buy a $400,000 house when, in fact, *they probably couldn't have afforded or decently qualified for a $100,000 home.* Unfortunately, within a year, he had passed away and the house was placed in foreclosure.

Now, don't get me wrong, **this couple had hearts of gold with a real desire to give and bless**. But, in this instance, *they personally made a large error in judgment* and *gave God the credit He didn't deserve or surely didn't want.*

**God never opens a door for failure in your life. You might, but He won't.**

There was a time in my life when I played poker, mostly because I was very good at it.

During one year of my life while I was on the national board of a civic organization ... *I traveled into 48 states a total of 120 times.* I would generally leave home with only pocket change and *finance my entire trip by playing poker.*

Would it be accurate to say that God made me successful in taking money from other folks? *I hardly think so.* I wasn't listening to Him like I should have been ... *back then.*

The last time I played for money was with a group of friends who worked in our insurance business when we were on a chartered plane trip. By this time I had come into a much closer relationship with the Lord. *After winning a substantial amount of money from them,* I was later convicted of my sin.

Upon my return home I wrote all of them a letter asking for their forgiveness and sent each one their money back. *I remember telling them that just because you're good at something doesn't mean you should do it.*

Sometimes in our deception ... *we credit God for things when He'd have nothing to do with it.*

**The only success God is going to give you is through those things that line up with His Word.**

However, it's critically important that we give God the glory for any and all successes that are manifested in our lives or in the lives of those we love.

God taught us this principle in Genesis 27:19-21 (NIV):

> *"Jacob said to his father, 'I am Esau your firstborn. I have done as you told me. Please sit*

*up and eat some of my game so that you may give me your blessing.' Isaac asked his son, 'How did you find it so quickly, my son?' 'The LORD your God gave me success,' he replied. Then Isaac said to Jacob, 'Come near so I can touch you, my son, to know whether you really are my son Esau or not.'"*

I always found it interesting that Jacob said, "The LORD <u>your</u> God gave me success." *He didn't say, "The Lord my God."* Instead he said, "Your God."

Jacob knew in his heart he was not right before God, *but he deceived his father anyway.*

If you further study this event, you'll find Jacob was swayed to deceive by the words of his own mother, Rebekah, *who took the curse upon herself (Genesis 27:12)* and *died while he was away* (although essentially, both she and Jacob suffered from the deception).

The interesting thing about deception … is that people generalize, rationalize and examine away many foolish decisions they make in their lives.

Having an affair because your spouse doesn't understand or appreciate you is the ultimate trick of the enemy. *God will not bring somebody into your life to destroy your marriage no matter how much they stroke your ego* or you think it needs stroking.

Here are six things you should know about deception.

## 1. Be aware: When you're being deceived you don't want to recognize the deception.

Jeremiah 9:6 in the New International Version says:

*"'You live in the midst of deception; in their deceit they refuse to acknowledge me,' declares the LORD."*

## 2. Deception always betrays those who live in it.

James 1:22 in the Amplified Bible says:

*"But be doers of the Word [obey the message], and not merely listeners to it, betraying yourselves [into deception by reasoning contrary to the Truth]."*

## 3. Recognize how you become deceived.

2 Corinthians 4:4 in the Amplified Bible says:

*"For the god of this world has blinded the unbelievers' minds [that they should not discern the truth], preventing them from seeing the illuminating light of the Gospel of the glory of Christ (the Messiah), Who is the Image and Likeness of God."*

## 4. Recognize who deceives you.

Genesis 3:13 says:

> *"Then the LORD God said to the woman, 'What is this you have done?' The woman said, 'The serpent deceived me, and I ate.'"*

## 5.      Only the truth will lead to your salvation.

2 Thessalonians 2:10 in the Amplified Bible says:

> *"And by unlimited seduction to evil and with all wicked deception for those who are perishing (going to perdition) because they did not welcome the Truth but refused to love it that they might be saved."*

## 6.      God is against every type of deception.

Proverbs 8:7 in the New Living Translation says:

> *"... for I speak the truth and detest every kind of deception."*

Financial deception is another favorite trick of the enemy.

Once again, I can't begin to tell you how many people have said to me:

> *"God knew what I needed when I needed it. He sent me this pre-approved offer for a new credit card."*

Child of God, let me assure you … *that's not God moving on your behalf*. That's an "angel of light" *coming to take your hard-earned money through a temporary "fix."* If you look into the spirit realm for just a moment, *you can see his pointy tail coming out of the envelope!*

Here's the bottom line … **God will NEVER give you success in any area that doesn't line up with His word**.

If you need wisdom … ask for it. James 1:5 in the Amplified Bible says:

> *"If any of you is deficient in wisdom, let him ask of the giving God [Who gives] to everyone liberally and ungrudgingly, without reproaching or faultfinding, and it will be given him."*

Finally, look at the wisdom found in James 3:17 in the Amplified Bible:

> *"But the wisdom from above is first of all pure (undefiled); then it is peace-loving, courteous (considerate, gentle). [It is willing to] yield to reason, full of compassion and good fruits; it is wholehearted and straightforward, impartial and unfeigned (free from doubts, wavering, and insincerity)."*

We must be watchful that we don't justify our personal *desires by claiming a divine intervention*. Instead, let's give God the credit for all the glorious things He's doing in our lives ... *many of which we take for granted* ... like the air that we breathe.

Let me look at everything ... honestly ... through your eyes. Thank you, Lord.

**Day 11**

# 10 Things About Being Poor

There is an old Chinese Proverb which says:

> "When you are poor, neighbors close by will not come; once you become rich, you'll be surprised by visits from relatives afar."

It reminded me of Ecclesiastes 9:15 in The Living Bible which says:

> *"Then I realized that though wisdom is better than strength, nevertheless, if the wise man is poor, he will be despised, and what he says will not be appreciated."*

As I was meditating on this verse, I felt impressed to write the "10 Things About Being Poor or Living In Lack."

## 1.    Being poor is not God's will for your life.

3 John 2 says:

> *"Beloved, I pray that you may prosper in every*

*way and [that your body] may keep well, even as*
*[I know] your soul keeps well and prospers."*

Psalm 23:1 in the Amplified Bible says:

*"THE LORD is my Shepherd [to feed, guide, and*
*shield me], I shall not lack."*

2 Chronicles 26:5 says:

*"… as long as he sought the LORD, God made*
*him to prosper."*

## 2.     Being poor doesn't make you holy.

Being poor doesn't make you holy any more than being rich makes you a saint. It's the condition of a person's heart, not the balance in their checkbook that
determines whether or not someone is holy.

Proverbs 21:17 in the New Living Translation says:

*"Those who love pleasure become poor; those*
*who love wine and luxury will never be rich."*

Being poor doesn't make you holy any more than going to Arby's makes you a roast beef sandwich.

Poverty is not be equated with holiness or righteousness.

Leviticus 20:7 in the Message Bible says:

*"Set yourselves apart for a holy life. Live a holy life, because I am God, your God. Do what I tell you; live the way I tell you. I am the God who makes you holy."*

## 3.　Being poor won't get you into heaven nor will it keep you out.

Some of the most evil people to ever draw a breath were born poor. The Word assures us that the ticket to heaven or ride up in the rapture will not be determined by whether or not we were poor.

Nor will being poor keep you out of heaven. Some of the greatest achievers in the world were also born poor.

However, poor people are not in a financial position to help fulfill the Great Commission or further Kingdom work … so, in effect, their poverty could keep other people out of heaven.

Again, our trip to heaven is not determined by whether we're poor or rich.

## 4.　Poor thinking is more hazardous to your financial health than actually being poor.

Proverbs 23:7 says:

*"As a man thinketh in his heart so is he …"*

Poor thinking is a self-perpetuating mentality with a

fatalistic view of your future financial possibilities. It's a "things are never going to change" view of your current existence.

## 5. Being poor doesn't make you a more effective person.

I heard someone say that a poor person has more time to do things effectively. The basic premise of such a statement is totally incorrect … if a poor person could do things more effectively … they wouldn't still be poor.

People who work hard become rich. Did I make that up? Nope, it's in the Word.

Proverbs 10:4 in the New Living Translation says:

*"Lazy people are soon poor; hard workers get rich."*

However, if you don't work hard … if you just sit back … you will suffer the economic consequences.

Proverbs 24:33-34 in the Message Bible says:

*"A nap here, a nap there, a day off here, a day off there, sit back, take it easy—do you know what comes next? Just this: You can look forward to a dirt-poor life, with poverty as your permanent houseguest!"*

## 6. Being poor doesn't make you a second-

**class citizen.**

Recently I was reading an article by Thomas Sowell, American economist and commentator, whom I really respect. He was talking about how poverty is viewed by certain people in the news media. He said:

> "Even in the United States, most people did not have a telephone or a refrigerator as late as 1930. Today, most Americans living below the official poverty level have not only these things but also color television, air-conditioning, a microwave oven, and a motor vehicle."

The definition of poor is totally different in other parts of the world. The World Bank defines poverty as someone living on less than $3 a day. This may seem ridiculous in the United States but there are over one billion people who live on less than a dollar a day.

According to Proverbs 22:2 in the New Living Translation, the rich and the poor, regardless of nationality, have one thing in common.

> *"The rich and poor have this in common: The Lord made them both."*

Not only did the Lord make both the rich and the poor but He is no respecter of persons. Throughout the scripture we're admonished to seek His wisdom and meditate on His Word so we can experience good success.

Joshua 1:8 in the New International Version spells out … how we do it.

> *"This set of instructions is not to cease being a part of your conversations. Meditate on it day and night, so that you may be careful to carry out everything that's written in it, for then you'll prosper and succeed."*

## 7.    Being proud of being poor is selfish and self-righteous.

I will always remember the man who with great pride told me that all he needed was enough money for himself and his family. I asked if he was serious about that statement and he emphatically said, "Yes." I proceeded to tell him that was the most selfish and unscriptural attitude that I'd heard in a long time.

I reminded him that the scripture tells us that we're to care for the widows and orphans.

James 1:27 says:

> *"Religion that pleases God the Father must be pure and spotless. You must help needy orphans and widows and not let this world make you evil."*

How can you care for the orphans and widows if you're so broke you can't pick up all the pieces?

## 8.    Being poor isn't permanent if you don't want

**it to be.**

I have often said that there is something much worse than being poor … it's to have a poor attitude.

Being poor is a temporary state … poor thinking is an attitude that oftentimes has been years in the making … thus filling your sub-conscious mind (your mental hard drive) with lots of negative and self-limiting thoughts. BUT GOD can change the way you think.

## 9. Being poor is expensive.

People who are poor are victimized on several levels. It costs money to be poor. Most banks are moving out of inner-city neighborhoods and check cashing services are moving in.

These services are designed to exploit poor people with high interest rates. Poor people seldom have checking accounts. They pay their bills with money orders which cost more than a good checking account when it's done month after month.

Sadly, there are people who are taking financial advantage of the poor and, scripturally speaking, that in itself is not a very smart thing to do.

Amos 8:4-6 in the Message Bible says:

*"Listen to this, you who walk all over the weak, you who treat poor people as less than nothing, Who say, 'When's my next paycheck coming so*

*I can go out and live it up?*

*"'How long till the weekend when I can go out and have a good time?' Who give little and take much, and never do an honest day's work. You exploit the poor, using them—and then, when they're used up, you discard them."*

## 10. Being poor is a magnet.

Without question, your financial attitude will draw to you … people who feel the way you do. You are either blessed or cursed by your associations.

Proverbs 13:20 in the Message Bible says:

*"Become wise by walking with the wise; hang out with fools and watch your life fall to pieces."*

People with negative and/or sinful behavior will try to bring you down to their level … they will never naturally seek to rise to your level.

1 Corinthians 15:33 in the Amplified Bible says:

*"Do not be so deceived and misled! Evil companionships (communion, associations) corrupt and deprave good manners and morals and character."*

By bringing you down … it's the only way they can feel good about themselves.

Proverbs 19:4 in the New Living Translation says:

*"Wealth makes many 'friends'; poverty drives them all away."*

# Day 12

# 7 Reasons to Fess Up If You Mess Up

It's okay to mess up … *if you confess what you've done, get up ... leave your pity party behind and begin moving on* to experience the rich and satisfying life God says can be yours through His Word.

Be warned right now ... *this teaching will directly impact your spiritual well-being and personal enrichment whether you realize it at first or not.*

**You may feel as though you've totally blown it in the past ... but God still has your back!** That statement is guaranteed in scripture. *It's not something I'm just saying to make you feel better.*

Here are seven reasons why it's okay if you've messed up in the past ...

## 1.    God will forgive your sins.

1 John 1:9 in the Amplified Bible says:

> *"If we [freely] admit that we have sinned and confess our sins, He is faithful and just (true to*

*His own nature and promises) and will forgive our sins [dismiss our lawlessness] and [continuously] cleanse us from all unrighteousness [everything not in conformity to His will in purpose, thought, and action]."*

Now that's what I call great news.

If we admit our sins and confess them … He will forgive us.

Not only that … but he will cleanse us from all unrighteousness.

What does 1 John 1:9 identify as unrighteousness?

*"… continuously] cleanse us from all unrighteousness [everything not in conformity to His will in purpose, thought, and action]."*

We're unrighteous … *not just because of the actions we take* but because of what we think about.

But Praise God … Hallelujah … He continuously cleanses us from unrighteousness.

## 2.  When you confess your sins … He will not deal harshly with you.

Psalm 103:10-12 in the New Living Translation says:

*"He does not punish us for all our sins; he does not deal harshly with us, as we deserve. For his*

*unfailing love toward those who fear him is as great as the height of the heavens above the earth. He has removed our sins as far from us as the east is from the west."*

Sometimes we beat ourselves up over our mistakes *more than anybody else ever would.*

## 3. When you pray for others ... dynamic and destiny-changing power is released into your life.

James 5:16 in the Amplified Bible says:

*"Confess to one another therefore your faults (your slips, your false steps, your offenses, your sins) and pray [also] for one another, that you may be healed and restored [to a spiritual tone of mind and heart]. The earnest (heartfelt, continued) prayer of a righteous man makes tremendous power available [dynamic in its working]."*

When we pray for one another ... *power is loosed in the spirit realm* ... and it's working in and through you.

Not only that ... Job 42:10 in the Amplified Bible says:

*"And the Lord turned the captivity of Job and restored his fortunes, when he prayed for his friends; also the Lord gave Job twice as much as he had before."*

When we pray for other people ... *we have ready access to dynamic power* ... everything the enemy has ever taken will be restored ... plus, we will have twice as much as we've ever had before.

## 4. God not only forgives your sins ... He forgets them as well.

Isaiah 43:25 in the Amplified Bible says:

*"I, even I, am He Who blots out and cancels your transgressions, for My own sake, and <u>I will not remember your sins.</u>"*

The Message Bible translation of Isaiah 43:25 says:

*"But I, yes I, am the one who takes care of your sins—that's what I do. <u>I don't keep a list of your sins.</u>"*

I remember hearing the story of a prophet who traveled to a particular city. His gift allowed him to read people's mail ... revealing things in their past, detailing things currently happening in their lives and giving a prophetic word for their future.

This one pastor who was planning to attend the meeting asked his wife to accompany him. She told him that she simply had too much to do. He persisted but she insisted it was not possible this time. Truth be told ... the pastor's wife was petrified that secrets from her past ... unknown to her husband ... would be revealed.

The pastor came home so pumped up after the meeting sharing everything that happened with his wife. She smiled and said, maybe next time I'll be able to go ... believing the prophet would not be coming again for many years.

Six months later the prophet came back to town and this time the pastor insisted his wife attend with him. No matter what she said ... he wouldn't take no for an answer. She reluctantly agreed provided they wouldn't have to sit in the preacher's section. She knew that visiting ministers almost always ministered to the preachers. Her husband agreed and they sat on the front row on the left-hand side ... the preachers being in the center section.

When he finished teaching ... the prophet announced that during his message God directed him not to minister to the pastors but to the people on the left-hand side of the church.

Can you imagine how the pastor's wife felt? She felt her worst fears were about to happen and the secrets of her past revealed to her husband and everyone else in the room.

When the prophet stepped in front of the pastor and his wife ... the pastor nudged his wife forward ... only to have the prophet say ... no, God is telling me something about your wife ... let me prophesy over you first.

The woman's heart sank ... she was horrified about

what she thought was most assuredly going to happen.

The prophet read her husband's mail ... revealing his past and giving him an encouraging word for the future. The pastor was in tears as the prophet called his wife forward.

The prophet told her the reason she was last was because God told him there was some serious sin in her past.

The room grew very quiet ... as all the saints slipped to the edge of their seats anticipating the prophet's next words ... inquiring minds wanting to know.

The woman could barely maintain her composure ... she was petrified of what was about to happen.

Everybody got quiet in anticipation ... the woman was barely breathing.

The prophet said, "So I asked God to reveal what your serious sin was. And God said," then the prophet paused before saying ... "I don't remember."

Child of God, your Heavenly Father not only forgives your sins ... He forgets them as well. It's time for you to do so as well.

**5.    Stop looking in the rearview mirror at your sins of the past.**

Isaiah 43:18 in the Message Bible says:

> *"Forget about what's happened: don't keep going over old history."*

The scripture is very clear about how God feels about those people who are looking back at past hurts, failures and sin. *It doesn't make Him happy.*

If you doubt what I've just said ... carefully read the words of Luke 9:62 in the Contemporary English Version:

> *"Jesus answered, 'Anyone who starts plowing and <u>keeps looking back isn't worth a thing</u> to God's kingdom!'"*

## 6.   God's not the One ... dropping a lot of guilt by your house.

If you've messed up ... not only does the enemy not want you confessing your sins ... *he wants to drop off an abundance of guilt from your past mistakes.*

Psalm 51:9 in the New Living Translation

> *"Don't keep looking at my sins. Remove the stain of my guilt."*

This particular trick of the devil can sometimes be overwhelming ... *because you keep looking at and rehearsing your past mistakes.*

*The number one key to removing guilt* is found in Psalm 51:10 in the New Living Translation which says:

> *"Create in me a clean heart, O God. Renew a loyal spirit within me."*

*Turn it over to God and let Him renew your spirit!*

One more verse. Isaiah 6:7 in the New Living Translation says:

> *"… Now your guilt is removed, and your sins are forgiven."*

Hallelujah and Amen!

## 7.  When you mess up your life … ask for His help and He'll become the most valuable player on your team.

Job 33:26 in the Message Bible says:

> *"Or, you may fall on your knees and pray—to God's delight! You'll see God's smile and celebrate, finding yourself set right with God. You'll sing God's praises to everyone you meet, testifying, 'I messed up my life— and let me tell you, it wasn't worth it. But God stepped in and saved me from certain death. I'm alive again! Once more I see the light!'"*

If you mess up … don't fret or freak out … confess

your sins and move on with what God has destined you to do.

# 7 Things God Really Hates

**Day 13**

## Have you ever thought about what God hates?

People who are familiar with the scriptures will think of Proverbs 6:16-19 as a principle example of what God hates.

*"These six things the Lord hates, indeed, seven are an abomination to Him: A proud look [the spirit that makes one overestimate himself and underestimate others], a lying tongue, and hands that shed innocent blood, A heart that manufactures wicked thoughts and plans, feet that are swift in running to evil, A false witness who breathes out lies [even under oath], and he who sows discord among his brethren."*

God hates …

1. A proud look … a spirit that overestimates himself and underestimates others.

2. A lying tongue. A half-truth is the same thing as

a whole lie.

3.      Hands that shed innocent blood.

4.      A heart that manufactures wicked thoughts and plans.

5.      People who run to or are anxious to engage in evil activities.

6.      A false witness … gives more meaning to the phrase "to tell the truth, the whole truth and nothing but the truth, so help you God."

7.      Sowing discord among brethren. *Notice there is no distinction between who is right and who is right* … who started the trouble *and who didn't*. This includes church families as well as blood relatives.

God has shown me a few other things He hates.

God hates it when His children worship other Gods (Deuteronomy 7:25; 12:29,31; 16:22).

God hates dishonesty, partiality and bribery (2 Chronicles 29:5).

God hates it when people cheat in business.

Proverbs 20:10 in the Message Bible says:

   *"Switching price tags and padding the expense*

*account are two things God hates."*

God's feelings on honest dealings are so strong His Word refers to it again in Proverbs 20:23 in the Message Bible which says:

*"God hates cheating in the marketplace ..."*

There is one other thing that God clearly hates and it's found in Psalm 119:113. In the New International Version it says:

*"I hate double-minded men ..."*

According to Strong's Concordance the word double-minded means:

**"a) wavering, uncertain, doubting
b) divided in interest."**

In the King James Version of Psalm 119:113 *double-minded is translated as "vain thoughts."*

I think it's clear that *God hates it when our minds are not stayed on ... focused on Him.* Obviously, in His infinite wisdom, *God considers a double-minded man to be a person who can't be trusted or relied on.*

James 1:8 in the Amplified Bible says:

*"[For being as he is] a man of two minds (hesitating, dubious, irresolute), [he is] unstable and unreliable and uncertain about everything [he*

*thinks, feels, decides]."*

God's Word tells us what He thinks … *His presence reveals what He feels and His instructions are the results of the decisions He made about how things ought to be.*

As a child if you wanted to please your earthly father then *you would be sensitive and obedient to how he thinks, feels and the decisions he's made. Our relationship with our Heavenly Father should be no different.*

Watching our favorite television show(s) into the night so we have just enough time to get up and out in the morning will not in any way allow us to understand God's divine nature and what He's thinking and feeling.

**The only way you and I can know what someone else is thinking and feeling is by spending time with them.** The fullness of our relationship with God is *determined by whether or not our loyalties are split between the things of this world and Him.*

James 1:8 in the New Living Translation says:

*"Their loyalty is divided between God and the world, and they are unstable in everything they do."*

**There is hope for those who are trying to walk with one foot in the world and another in the**

**Word.**

James 4:8 in the New International Version says:

*"Come near to God and he will come near to you. Wash your hands, you sinners, and purify your hearts, you double-minded."*

The way to please God … and think like He thinks *is to set our minds on Him.*

Romans 8:5 in the Amplified Bible says:

*"For those who are according to the flesh and are controlled by its unholy desires set their minds on and pursue those things which gratify the flesh, but those who are according to the Spirit and are controlled by the desires of the Spirit set their minds on and seek those things which gratify the [Holy] Spirit."*

**When your mind is fixed and stayed on the Lord, *then He will become your personal bodyguard.***

Isaiah 26:3 in the Amplified Bible says:

*"You will guard him and keep him in perfect and constant peace whose mind [both its inclination and its character] is stayed on You, because he commits himself to You, leans on You, and hopes confidently in You."*

*If you're experiencing personal turbulence in your life*

*at the moment,* then Isaiah 26:3 in the New Living Translation *will tell you how to find the calm that you desire.*

*"You will keep in perfect peace all who trust in you, all whose thoughts are fixed on you!"*

**Here's a revelation … <u>you're the only one who can keep you from being double-minded</u> …** *it's a matter of choice.*

*You will either activate the principles of God by thinking as He thinks or you'll live a life going from crisis to crisis.*

1 Peter 1:13 in the New International Version says:

*"Therefore, prepare your minds for action; be self-controlled; set your hope fully on the grace to be given you when Jesus Christ is revealed."*

There comes a point in all of our lives *when we know that we know what we ought to be doing.* Then it's a matter of doing it.

1 Peter 1:13-16 in the Message Bible says:

*"So roll up your sleeves, put your mind in gear, be totally ready to receive the gift that's coming when Jesus arrives. Don't lazily slip back into those old grooves of evil, doing just what you feel like doing. You didn't know any better then; you do now. As obedient children, let yourselves*

*be pulled into a way of life shaped by God's life, a life energetic and blazing with holiness. God said, 'I am holy; you be holy.'"*

This is especially true when it comes to debt. Buying stuff we don't need with money we don't have to *impress people who couldn't really care less about you* and the state of your financial affairs and spiritual life … is not spiritually or financially wise.

Buying stuff will never give us the peace of mind. *Living a life focused on what He thinks and feels will.*

**In the final analysis, it's simple … our mind is focused on Him or it's not.**

Have you ever asked someone you loved … someone you were trying to have a conversation with … where their mind is focused?

You were simply wanting to know what or who they were thinking about because *it's obvious you were not the object of their thought process at that very moment.* God wants us thinking about Him

Colossians 3:2 in the Amplified Bible says:

*"And set your minds and keep them set on what is above (the higher things), not on the things that are on the earth."*

Deuteronomy 32:46 in the Amplified Bible says:

*"He said to them, Set your [minds and] hearts on*

*all the words which I command you this day, that you may command them to your children, that they may be watchful to do all the words of this law."*

I think it's clear where God wants our minds to be … and what He wants us to do.

# Day 14

## 12 Things About Abigail

There are 12 amazing characteristics about Abigail who became a wife to King David.

1 Samuel 25:2-3 says:

> *"And there was a man in Maon (my own), whose possessions were in Carmel (kcare mel); and the man was very great, and he had three thousand sheep, and a thousand goats: and he was shearing his sheep in Carmel.*

> *"Now the name of the man was Nabal (na vall); and the name of his wife Abigail: and she was a woman of good understanding, and of a beautiful countenance: but the man was churlish and evil in his doings; and he was of the house of Caleb."*

The first two things we discover about her:

1.    **Abigail was wise ... she had good understanding.**

2.    **Abigail was beautiful.**

So the immediate question is ... *why would a smart, good-looking woman marry somebody whose name, Nabal, means fool. Why marry a man who is described in the scriptures as crude and mean in all his dealings?*

The scripture doesn't give us the answer ... *but the biblical times indicate it was an arranged marriage, which was very common.* Nabal was a wealthy man and he *probably offered a pretty good dowry to marry someone as fine as Abigail.*

## 3. Abigail didn't fret or panic when she received disturbing news.

In the scripture we read that David and his mighty men are out in the same fields where Nabal's men were watching his flocks. *David provided a wall of protection for them so that nothing was missing or harmed.*

Sheep-shearing time was a time of celebration so David sends messengers to Nabal to ask if he and his men might join in on the festivities; however, David's men are dismissed gruffly.

Thus in 1 Samuel 25:17, a servant who overhears Nabal's retort runs to Abigail for advice:

> *"Now therefore know and consider what thou wilt do; for evil is determined against our master, and against all his household ..."*

**4.    Abigail took immediate action in a difficult situation**.

1 Samuel 25:18 says:

*"Then Abigail made haste …"*

**5.    Abigail understood the family finances and the value of giving.**

1 Samuel 25:18 says:

*"… and took two hundred loaves, and two bot-tles of wine, and five sheep ready dressed, and five measures of parched corn, and an hundred clusters of raisins, and two hundred cakes of figs, and laid them on (donkeys) asses."*

**6.    Abigail considered all the obstacles to her plan and took action to minimize them.**

1 Samuel 25:19 says:

*"And she said unto her servants, Go on before me; behold, I come after you. But she told not her husband Nabal."*

**7.    Abigail understood honor and gave respect where it was due.**

1 Samuel 25:23-24 says:

*"And when Abigail saw David, she hasted, and*

*lighted off the (donkey) ass, and fell before David on her face, and bowed herself to the ground, And fell at his feet, and said, Upon me, my lord, upon me let this iniquity be: and let thine handmaid, I pray thee, speak in thine audience, and hear the words of thine handmaid."*

## 8.    Abigail didn't ignore or blame Nabal or anyone else for the problem.

1 Samuel 25:27-29 says:

*"And now this blessing which thine handmaid hath brought unto my lord, let it even be given unto the young men that follow my lord. I pray thee, forgive the trespass of thine handmaid: for the LORD will certainly make my lord a sure house; because my lord fighteth the battles of the LORD, and evil hath not been found in thee all thy days."*

By the way, it would have been easy for Abigail to imply that this was not her fault *because she didn't want to marry this loser in the first place. But she used the wisdom of God instead of the excuses of man so David could be the judge.*

## 9.    Abigail used her wisdom to point out the problems with David's intended plan of action.

1 Samuel 25:31 says:

*"That this shall be no grief unto thee, nor offence*

*of heart unto my lord, either that thou hast shed blood causeless, or that my lord hath avenged himself: but when the LORD shall have dealt well with my lord, then remember thine hand-maid."*

**10. The evidence of Abigail's wisdom and honor prevented intended harm from coming to her house.**

1 Samuel 25:33-34 in the Amplified Bible says:

*"And blessed be your discretion and advice, and blessed be you who have kept me today from blood guiltiness and from avenging myself with my own hand. For as the Lord, the God of Israel, lives, Who has prevented me from hurting you, if you had not hurried and come to meet me, sure-ly by morning there would not have been left so much as one male to Nabal."*

**11. Abigail took her hands off the situation and trusted God to deal with Nabal.**

1 Samuel 25:37-38 says:

*"But it came to pass in the morning, when the wine was gone out of Nabal, and his wife had told him these things, that his heart died within him, and he became as a stone. And it came to pass about ten days after, that the LORD smote Nabal, that he died."*

## 12. Abigail found that right thinking and actions bring a reward.

1 Samuel 25:39-41 says:

*"And when David heard that Nabal was dead, he said, Blessed be the LORD, that hath pleaded the cause of my reproach from the hand of Nabal, and hath kept his servant from evil: for the LORD hath returned the wickedness of Nabal upon his own head. And David sent and communed with Abigail, to take her to him to wife. And when the servants of David were come to Abigail to Carmel, they spake unto her, saying, David sent us unto thee, to take thee to him to wife. And she arose, and bowed herself on her face to the earth, and said, Behold, let thine handmaid be a servant to wash the feet of the servants of my lord."*

I want to look at the fifth point again.

**Abigail also understood the family finances and the value of giving.**

Sadly, there are some women who are married to husbands who are more like *knuckleheads or if you prefer, Nabals,* in that they are foolish ... spiritually, financially and otherwise.

**<u>Financial foolishness is not gender specific</u>**; however, studies show that men are more prone to impulse buying than women.

Abigail is described as *wise and it takes wisdom to know where submission ends and sin begins*. For instance, a wife should never sign a federal income tax return that she knows is fraudulent … because that is ethically wrong … it is sin.

Over the years I've talked with hundreds, if not thousands, of women whose husbands refuse to have them tithe and/or give offerings.

My advice is simple, **if you have a job then tithe on the money you make**. You're accountable for the tithe on that money and not your husband's.

I know women who are what some call housewives but I call them household executives. They don't work *outside but inside the home and they have saved money from groceries and other expenditures in order to tithe and give offerings*. I know women who have made baked goods or other things to sell so they would have money to give to God.

God understands your heart … *your desire to give* … seek God and let Him direct your path … *no matter how difficult the situation may seem* … if it worked for Abigail, it will work for you.

# Day 15

## 5 Seeds for 5 Needs

It's been said that a seed meets every need … that's so true. In fact, Bishop Keith Butler wrote a great book titled, *A Seed Meets Every Need.* My personal friend and mentor Dr. Mike Murdock says that everything in life is a seed.

Let's talk about five Bible stories where people had a very specific need … all of which were met by a seed.

### First, let's look at the woman with the alabaster box.

Luke 7:36-37 says:

> *"And one of the Pharisees desired him that he would eat with him. And he went into the Pharisee's house, and sat down to meat. And, behold, a woman in the city, which was a sinner, when she knew that Jesus sat at meat in the Pharisee's house, brought an alabaster box of ointment."*

Matthew 26:7 says the alabaster box contained very precious ointment. You can be assured that whatever was in that box wasn't cheap and it didn't come from the Dollar Store. In fact, verse 7 in the New Living Translation said it was "very expensive."

Luke 7:46 says:

*"My head with oil thou didst not anoint: but this woman hath anointed my feet with ointment."*

The Amplified Bible translation of Luke 7:46 says:

*"You didn't anoint my head with [cheap, ordinary] oil, but she has anointed my feet with [expensive, rare] perfume."*

Luke 7:47-50 says:

*"Wherefore I say unto thee, Her sins, which are many, are forgiven; for she loved much: but to whom little is forgiven, the same loveth little. And he said unto her, Thy sins are forgiven. And they that sat at meat with him began to say within themselves, Who is this that forgiveth sins also? And he said to the woman, Thy faith hath saved thee; go in peace."*

**It's important to notice that Jesus said the woman's giving was an act of faith.** He also pointed out that she came with expensive perfume, ready to wash his feet. As a result, her need was met. *Her need was to be forgiven.*

Verse 38 says she *"… stood at His feet before Him*

weeping ..." Now look at last sentence of verse 39, where it tells us ... *"she is a sinner."*

It is important to see and understand what happened here ... the woman brought precious ointment—a seed of monetary value to worship Jesus ... and she walked out with her sins forgiven.

## **The second scriptural example I want to share of a seed meeting a specific need is that of Zacchaeus.**

Luke 19:1-9 says:

*"And Jesus entered and passed through Jericho. And, behold, there was a man named Zacchaeus, which was the chief among the publicans, and he was rich. And he sought to see Jesus who he was; and could not for the press, because he was little of stature. And he ran before, and climbed up into a sycamore tree to see him: for he was to pass that way. And when Jesus came to the place, he looked up, and saw him, and said unto him, Zacchaeus, make haste, and come down; for to day I must abide at thy house. And he made haste, and came down, and received him joyfully. And when they saw it, they all murmured, saying, That he was gone to be guest with a man that is a sinner. And Zacchaeus stood, and said unto the Lord; Behold, Lord, the half of my goods I give to the poor; and if I have taken any thing from any man by false accusation, I restore him fourfold."*

Zacchaeus was saying, "Hey Lord, I'm rich, I'm going to give half of what I've got to the poor and if I've cheated anyone, I will pay them back four times the value of what I stole."

Zacchaeus didn't need money … he had plenty of it. How many of you know that if Bill Gates were to give half of his money to the poor … he'd still have enough money left to be rich? Giving to the poor and the four-fold restoration were seeds that Zacchaeus was sowing to show repentance for the wrong he had done. He didn't need money … but he did need salvation.

Luke 19:9 says:

*"And Jesus said unto him, This day is salvation come to this house, forsomuch as he also is a son of Abraham."*

Zacchaeus seed met his need which was salvation.

## Our third example of a seed meeting a need is that of the Centurion.

Luke 7:1-5 says:

*"Now when he had ended all his sayings in the audience of the people, he entered into Caper-naum. And a certain centurion's servant, who was dear unto him, was sick, and ready to die. And when he heard of Jesus, he sent unto him the elders of the Jews, beseeching him that he would come and heal his servant. And when*

*they came to Jesus, they besought him instantly, saying, That he was worthy for whom he should do this: For he loveth our nation, and he hath built us a synagogue."*

The Amplified Bible translation of Luke 7:5 says:

*"For he loves our nation and built us a synagogue [at his own expense]."*

The Centurion was wealthy enough to build the children of Israel a synagogue with his own money. Can you imagine how unusual this was? A Roman Centurion built a meeting place for the Jewish people out of his own money.

Luke 7:6-8 says:

*"Then Jesus went with them. And when he was now not far from the house, the centurion sent friends to him, saying unto him, Lord, trouble not thyself: for I am not worthy that thou shouldest enter under my roof: Wherefore neither thought I myself worthy to come unto thee: but say in a word, and my servant shall be healed. For I also am a man set under authority, having under me soldiers, and I say unto one, Go, and he goeth; and to another, Come, and he cometh; and to my servant, Do this, and he doeth it."*

The Centurion believed if Jesus just spoke the word that his servant would be healed.

Luke 7:9 says:

*"When Jesus heard these things, he marvelled at him, and turned him about, and said unto the people that followed him, I say unto you, I have not found so great faith, no, not in Israel."*

What put this man in a position for his need to be met—was his seed. Yet, he didn't sow this seed for his financial need … he sowed a seed for his servant to be healed.

## The fourth example is the man with palsy and his four faithful friends.

Mark 2:1-4 says:

*"And again he entered into Capernaum, after some days; and it was noised that he was in the house. And straightway many were gathered to-gether, insomuch that there was no room to re-ceive them, no, not so much as about the door: and he preached the word unto them. And they come unto him, bringing one sick of the palsy, which was borne of four. And when they could not come nigh unto him for the press, they un-covered the roof where he was: and when they had broken it up, they let down the bed wherein the sick of the palsy lay."*

Trying to get into that house would be like trying to get into a Benny Hinn meeting after the doors had just been opened but *these four friends were determined.*

One of the four got the bright idea of tearing a hole in the roof and *lowering the sick man and his bed* down through the roof to Jesus.

First, it *must not have been a small house*. There had to be enough room to tear a hole big enough to lower a man down into just one room. I want you to get this … if you tear the roof off somebody's house … you are going to have **to pay to have it fixed**. If you come to my house and tear a hole in my roof … you are going to have to fix it.

These men knew they would have to pay to have the roof fixed … but it didn't hold them back. These men were willing to pay *whatever price* … to meet the need of their friend. They knew their actions were going to cost them some money … but they were willing to *do whatever was necessary to have the needs* of their friend met.

The Bible records that upon seeing their faith, Jesus said to the man on the stretcher, *"Your sins are forgiven thee,"* and in verse 11, *"take up thy bed and walk."*

These men sowed a seed to meet the need of a friend.

**Our fifth and final example is the Old Testament story of the Queen of Sheba.**

The Queen of Sheba had heard about the wisdom and wealth of King Solomon … so she paid him a visit. She came to see for herself if Solomon was real by asking him hard questions … but she didn't come to him empty-handed … she took a seed.

1 Kings 10:1-3 says:

> *"And when the queen of Sheba heard of the fame of Solomon concerning the name of the Lord, she came to prove him with hard questions. And she came to Jerusalem with a very great train, with camels that bare spices, and very much gold, and precious stones: and when she was come to Solomon, she communed with him of all that was in her heart. And Solomon told her all her questions: there was not any thing hid from the king, which he told her not."*

The Queen of Sheba was serious about wisdom so she *brought serious seed*. She needed wisdom and understanding on how to run her country. *Nothing was hidden from Solomon so he could provide her with all her answers.*

The Queen's seed brought her wisdom and understanding and gave her the *opportunity to spend time with the greatest man of her time* and truthfully of all time except for Jesus.

Proverbs 18:16 says:

> *"A man's gift maketh room for him and bringeth him before great men."*

The Queen's seed **brought her in front of a great man** so she could *understand how he ruled his king-dom*. She left for home with wisdom but much more. Solomon told her **to take anything out of the royal bounty** that she wanted. Can you imagine how much bounty there was?

In these five examples ... we've seen *five seeds meet five different needs ... forgiveness, salvation, the healing of a friend*, the need of a friend being met and a seed for divine connection.

**A seed will meet any need.**

# Day 16

## 7 Features of Your God-Given GPS

Daniel Boone, the American fron-tiersman, humorously said he was never lost but he was bewildered once for three days and nights.

*If you don't know where you're going, then you find it's easier to get lost or sidetracked along the way.*

Today, every smartphone comes with GPS. *Technology has not only made GPS more affordable* ... it is also more sophisticated. The change has been amazing.

Recently, I was sitting in an Alamo rental car bus being transported from their lot to the airport terminal. I had to smile as I read a sign in the bus which said:

**"Get directions from satellites not just gas stations."**

As I was thinking on those words ... I suddenly realized that believers have a built-in GPS.

Here are seven amazing features about your God-given GPS.

**First, your GPS is _God's Positioning System_.**

Genesis 3:9 in the New International Version asks a powerful question ... one that demands an answer from each of us. The verse says:

> *"But the Lord God called to the man, 'Where are you?'"*

I'm sure this is not surprise to you but *God knew where Adam was and He knew why he was there.*

So when God asked, "Where are you?" ... *it was much more than a geographical question.*

**God is asking us the same question today ... *He wants to know where you are in fulfilling His purposes for your life ... your calling ... and the goals He's directed you to achieve.***

Adam had violated God's instructions ... *dishonored God's word ... yielded to temptation ... he had been given unlimited potential and was enjoying all the benefits God had given him but he chose disobedience.*

Does any of that sound familiar? ... are we doing what God created us to do ... *being all that we can be* to bring honor to the kingdom as we enjoy all His blessings?

*You may be living in the land of mediocrity … but God wants you traveling forward into your land flowing with milk and honey.*

## Second, your GPS is *God's Protection System*.

Have you ever seen in the movies or on television where *a criminal would offer to provide protection to a local merchant for a specified amount of money each week?* Generally, *the only one threatening the merchant was the one doing the protecting.*

You and I have a protection from all adversaries beyond anything the world has ever seen … *and it's ours for the receiving.*

Psalm 5:11 in the New Living Translation says:

> *"But let all who take refuge in you be glad; let them ever sing for joy. Spread your protection over them that those who love your name may rejoice in you."*

Not only does God offer you protection … but your enemies become His enemies.

Exodus 23:22 in the Amplified Bible says:

> *"But if you will indeed listen to and obey His voice … I will be an enemy to your enemies and an adversary to your adversaries."*

*God's Protection System is better, more thorough and*

*less expensive monetarily than those offered by ADT or Brinks Home Security Systems.*

**Third, your GPS is _God's Peace System_.**

I never cease to be amazed at how *much God loves us*. He sent His only begotten Son to give us abundant life now and throughout eternity.

As a natural father *I always want to comfort my daughters or sons when they are troubled or concerned* ... I desire to help them with an inner peace so they can be free of fear and worry.

When Jesus left Planet Earth ... He gave us a powerful gift ... found in John 14:27 which says:

> *"Peace I leave with you, my peace I give unto you: not as the world giveth, give I unto you. Let not your heart be troubled, neither let it be afraid."*

The Lord will give you His strength *and peace in the midst of every adversity.*

**Fourth, your GPS is _God's Promotion System_.**

Have you ever been promoted?

From one grade to the next in school ... *from one level of accomplishment to the next in the Boy or Girl Scouts ... from one rank to a higher one in the military or from one position to a different one at your place of employment? Or from owning one store to opening another?*

If you think the promotion was a result of your skills and/or your hard work … then I suggest you read, study and meditate on Psalm 75:6 in the Message Bible:

*"For promotion and power come from nowhere on earth, but only from God. He promotes one and deposes another."*

Your promotion comes from the Lord. **He gives you the power and favor for advancement in every single area of human endeavor.**

**Fifth, your GPS is _God's Possibility System_.**

Let's immediately establish one fact … with and through God all things are possible.

Matthew 19:26 says:

*"But Jesus beheld them, and said unto them, With men this is impossible; but with God all things are possible."*

Mark 9:23 in the God's Word Translation says:

*"Jesus said to him, 'As far as possibilities go, everything is possible for the person who believes.'"*

The enemy of your success and prosperity does not want you thinking in terms of possibilities … he wants you practicing an "impossibility mentality" instead of the "unlimited possibilities mentality" God gave you.

Luke 1:37 says:

*"For with God nothing shall be impossible."*

If something is impossible it was your choice.

Matthew 17:20 says:

*"And Jesus said unto them, Because of your unbelief: for verily I say unto you, If ye have faith as a grain of mustard seed, ye shall say unto this mountain, Remove hence to yonder place; and it shall remove; and nothing shall be impossible unto you."*

Repeat those last six words with me.

**"… nothing shall be impossible unto you."**

Now personalize that … *"Nothing shall be impossible to <<your name>>." (Raymond, Darrell, Caroline)*

**Sixth, your GPS is _God's Power System_.**

I'm about to speak a five-word sentence … *the reality of which can change your life forever.* Here it is:

**God hasn't left you powerless.**

Acts 1:8 says:

> *"… ye shall receive power, after that the Holy Ghost is come upon you … (then) ye shall become witnesses …"*

The power Jesus promises after the Holy Ghost comes upon you is *enabling power*.

The Greek word for power is dunamis which means:

## **"ability."**

So let's look at this verse again as I expand the paraphrase for you.

> *"You shall receive the ability after the Holy Ghost has come upon you, and you will be able to witness of me simultaneously in Jerusalem, and in Judea, and in Samaria, and to the uttermost parts of the earth."*

## Seven, your GPS is *God's Prosperity System*.

Here are seven scriptural reasons why God wants you to prosper.

Deuteronomy 8:18 in the Amplified Bible says:

> *"But you shall [earnestly] remember the Lord your God, for it is He Who gives you power to get wealth, that He may establish His covenant which He swore to your fathers, as it is this day."*

Job 36:11 says:

> *"If they obey and serve him, they shall spend their days in prosperity, and their years in pleasures."*

1 Kings 2:3 in the Amplified Bible says:

> *"Keep the charge of the Lord your God, walk in His ways, keep His statutes, His commandments, His precepts, and His testimonies, as it is written in the Law of Moses, that you may do wisely and prosper in all that you do and wherever you turn."*

And finally … here are two scriptures that tell you exactly what you must do to prosper.

Joshua 1:8 in the Amplified Bible says:

> *"This Book of the Law shall not depart out of your mouth, but you shall meditate on it day and night, that you may observe and do according to all that is written in it. For then you shall make your way prosperous, and then you shall deal wisely and have good success."*

2 Chronicles 26:5 says:

> *"… as long as he sought the LORD, God made him to prosper."*

Now it's time for you to fully activate your personal

God-given GPS to take you places God has already ordained for you … but you've only dreamed of.

## Day 17

# 7 Things You Don't Want the Enemy to Know

Here are seven things YOU don't want the enemy to know.

## 1. When you're disappointed.

Here's the great news … regardless of the intensity of the enemy's attack … *you will never be put to shame or disappointed*. I realize that's a bold statement … but consider the *following verse in the Amplified Bible translation.*

Psalm 25:3 in the Amplified Bible says:

> *"Yes, let none who trust and wait hopefully and look for You be put to shame or be disappointed; let them be ashamed who forsake the right or deal treacherously without cause."*

Psalm 25:20 in the Amplified Bible says the same thing.

> *"Guard my soul and rescue me; Do not let me be ashamed or disappointed, For I have taken refuge in You."*

God is going to <u>make sure you're not disappointed</u>. Not only that, *He will reward you for what you've been through.*

Proverbs 23:18 in the New Living Translation says:

*"You will be rewarded for this; your hope will not be disappointed."*

## 2.    When you're afraid.

Never let the devil or any of his demon horde see you when you're afraid … in fact, the scripture tells us *26 times in the King James Version of the Bible to "be not afraid."*

*There are **44 verses in the Message Bible that say "Don't be afraid"** and 66 verses in the New Living Translation* with the exact same scriptural directive for us.

*One reason you don't have to be afraid is because you're not the one fighting the battle …* alone.

2 Chronicles 20:15 says:

*"… Thus saith the LORD unto you, Be not afraid nor dismayed by reason of this great multitude; for the battle is not yours, but God's."*

You don't have to be afraid of *what you see.*

You don't have to be afraid of *what you've heard.*

2 Kings 19:6 says:

> *"… Be not afraid of the words which thou hast heard …"*

Mark 5:36 says:

> *"… Be not afraid, only believe."*

## 3.     When you don't know what to do.

When you're not sure what to do next … God not only knows what to do … He will tell you what to do.

Proverbs 3:5-6 in the Message Bible says:

> *"Trust God from the bottom of your heart; don't try to figure out everything on your own. Listen for God's voice in everything you do, everywhere you go; he's the one who will keep you on track."*

If you're in the *midst of a storm or financial firefight* and you don't know what to do next *"… don't try to figure it out on your own …"*

**If you're trying to figure things out … to solve your problems by yourself … then you don't need God.**

As the verse says, you must *"… listen for God's voice in everything you do …"*

## 4.     When you've spent every cent you've got.

God reminded me of His biblical solution for *our mistakes* of bad judgment.

James 5:16 says:

> *"Confess your faults one to another, and pray one for another, that ye may be healed [the fault removed] …"*

When we fall into the devil's trap of purchasing things we regret, *we become the possessors of what Jesus calls "sycamine trees."*

In Luke 17:6 the scripture says:

> *"And the Lord said, if ye had faith as a grain of mustard seed, ye might say unto this sycamine tree, Be thou plucked up by the root, and be thou planted in the sea; and it shall obey you."*

I can hear you saying, "Brother Harold, what makes you think my regrettable purchases are like a sycamine tree?"

It becomes clearer when you see the definition of *sycamine in the Greek.* It is the word sykaminos (G4807) and *means:*

### *"an imitation mulberry tree."*

It looks like it will produce fruit, but produces none.

*When you mistakenly spend your hard-earned money*

*for products or services that turn out to be an imitation of God's best for you, my friend you have been sold a sycamine tree!*

## 5. When the doctor gives you a bad report.

Have you ever known someone who speaks with absolute authority but does so without the basis of all the facts?

**When a doctor gives you a bad report ...** *he/she can only tell you the facts they perceive based on their experiences and training.*

In essence, they're spreading a bad report *without knowing the truth*. Such proclamations can undermine the confidence of those who should know better. And yes, such announcements will cause you to worry ... *if you don't have a firm grasp of the truth found in God's Word.*

**You can have facts without having the truth.**

For instance, the ten spies came back to Moses with a bad report. They brought back the facts as they perceived them to be. They brought an evil report that made all the others sweat about what lay ahead of them.

Numbers 13:32 in the New Century Version says:

> *"And those men gave the Israelites a bad report about the land they explored, saying, 'The land*

*that we explored is too large to conquer. All the people we saw are very tall."'*

Numbers 14:36 in the New Century Version says:

*"The men Moses had sent to explore the land had returned and spread complaints among all the people. They had given a bad report about the land."*

The ten spies who brought back the bad report suffered the consequences for believing facts over the truth when it didn't line up with God's Word.

Numbers 14:37 in the New Living Translation says:

*"These men who were responsible for spreading the bad report about the land were struck down and died of a plague before the LORD."*

The doctor may give you a bad report … he may give you the facts he knows … but don't sweat it because you have the truth.

## 6.    When someone you love is doing or has done something stupid.

Despite your best efforts as a parent … your children will do some unwise (or let's call it what it is … stupid) things. Here's what you need to know.

### First, God is still on the throne.

Psalm 45:46 in the English Standard Version says:

*"Your throne, O God, is forever and ever. The scepter of your kingdom is a scepter of uprightness."*

**Second, Jesus came to deliver you and your family from the devil's hold.**

Hebrews 2:4 says:

*"God also bearing them witness, both with signs and wonders, and with divers miracles, and gifts of the Holy Ghost, according to his own will ..."*

**Third, God doesn't want anyone in your family to spend an eternity in hell.**

2 Peter 3:9 in The Amplified Bible tell us:

*"The Lord does not delay [as though He were unable to act] and is not slow about His promise, as some count slowness, but is [extraordinarily] patient toward you, not wishing for any to perish but for all to come to repentance."*

**Fourth, God not only forgives our sins, foolishness and stupidity ... but He forgets them as well.**

Isaiah 43:25 in The Message translation says:

*"But I, yes I, am the one who takes care of your sins—that's what I do. <u>I don't keep a list of your sins</u>."*

**Fifth, God will give you hope for your children as they move into a relationship with Him.**

Psalm 112:1-3 in The Message translation tells us:

*"Hallelujah! Blessed man, blessed woman, who fear God, who cherish and relish his commandments, their children robust on the earth, and the homes of the upright—how blessed! Their houses brim with wealth and a generosity that never runs dry."*

**Sixth, your kids who once frustrated you ... will now receive a generational blessing because the enemy never saw you sweat over their future.**

Genesis 22:18 in the English Standard Version says:

*"And <u>in your offspring shall all the nations of the earth be blessed</u>, because you have obeyed my voice."*

**7.     When you're advancing behind enemy lines.**

As I wrote that line I began to think of the Integrity Music chorus that says:

**"I went to the enemy's camp and took back what he stole from me."**

Here are seven indisputable reasons why you can take back what the enemy has stolen from you.

### First, you're not alone.

Deuteronomy 20:1 says:

*"When thou goest out to battle against thine enemies, and seest horses, and chariots, and a people more than thou, be not afraid of them: for the Lord thy God is with thee, which brought thee up out of the land of Egypt."*

### Second, you're not going to fight the battle.

2 Chronicles 20:15 says:

*"... Thus saith the LORD unto you, Be not afraid nor dismayed by reason of this great multitude; for the battle is not yours, but God's."*

### Third, there is only one thing you have to do.

Mark 5:36 says:

*"... Be not afraid, only believe."*

**Fourth, if you're going to face your enemies … call in reinforcements.**

Psalm 118:5-6 in the New International Version tells us:

*"When hard pressed, I cried to the Lord; he brought me into a spacious place. The Lord is with me; I will not be afraid. What can mere mortals do to me?"*

**Fifth, anyone who opposes you, opposes Him.**

Exodus 23:22 says:

*"But if you will indeed listen to and obey His voice … I will be an enemy to your enemies and an adversary to your adversaries."*

**Sixth, you will come out of the battle unharmed.**

Psalm 118:6 in the Message Bible says:

*"… who would dare lay a hand on me?"*

**Seventh, you've got protection stronger than Superman's cape or Spiderman's web.**

Hebrews 13:5-6 in the Amplified Bible says:

*"So we take comfort and are encouraged and confidently and boldly say, The Lord is my Helper; I will not be seized with alarm [I will not fear or dread or be terrified]. What can*

*man do to me?"*

Never allow the enemy to know when he's hit you in a weak or vunerable spot ... instead call on and out the heavy artillery ... the Word of God and you'll win every victory.

Don't let the enemy know what you're thinking and feeling ... but always talk things over with God.

When you know the truth ... you need to act on it.

**Day 18**

## Is Your Price Right?

Have you ever played "The Price Is Right?"

Truthfully, I'm **amused and amazed** by how foolish some people will act on national television *but yet they're too refined to jump up screaming and run around a church* where God set them free of sin and death.

What's your price?

Do you have a price to *act foolish in front of others?*

Do you have a price to *compromise your principles?*

Do you have a price to *accept less than the best?*

**Do you fully understand the consequences of the price that you're being asked to pay for this or that?**

There are millions of believers and other folks who are suffering through the bondage of debt because they had a price. The vendor/creditor/*debt maker* en-hanced the offer to make it seem irresistible.

Perhaps you experienced the Don Corlene mentality. *You were made an offer you couldn't seemingly refuse*.

**So here's the question:**

Do you have a price for your *values?* For your *friends?* For your *soul?* For your *life?*

**Judas did.** We found the account in Mark 14:10-11:

> *"And Judas Iscariot, one of the twelve, went unto the chief priests, to betray him unto them. And when they heard it, they were glad, and promised to give him money. And he sought how he might conveniently betray him."*

Judas was motivated by greed … but he was also motivated by *pride and jealousy*.

Let's establish that thirty pieces of silver was *a significant amount of money at the time in biblical history* … it was roughly $950 … which is **the equivalent of $240,000 today according to the Professional Coin Grading Service.**

What can you do with $240,000?

You could buy *two brand new Mercedes S500s.*

You could make a ten percent down payment *on a $2.4 million house.*

There is no question that $240,000 is a lot of money to most of us … but to other people it's just chump change. Do you think that $240,000 would be the price for men like Bill Gates or Warren Buffet? *Of course not.*

I find it interesting that the Pharisees didn't even blink when Judas told them the price. The scripture says: *"… when they heard it, they were glad."*

The price was obviously something they could well afford. **But I want you to consider another point.**

Jesus traveled with a large contingent of people who had to beefed and cared for. **A significant amount of money must have flowed through the ministry to handle all the various accommodations.**

*The scripture says that Judas was a thief* … and as such *he was ripping off the treasury.* John 12:4 in The Amplified Bible tells us:

> *"But Judas Iscariot, the one of His disciples who was about to betray Him, said, Why was this perfume not sold for 300 denarii [a year's wages for an ordinary workman] and that [money] given to the poor (the destitute)? Now he did not say this because he cared for the poor but because he was a thief; and having the bag (the money box, the purse of the Twelve), he took for himself what was put into it [pilfering the collections]."*

The Message Bible translation of verse 6 says:

> "... He was in charge of their common funds, but also embezzled them."

While I can't prove it this side of heaven ... I'm confident *Judas was in a position to significantly steal more than thirty pieces of silver.*

I don't think greed or money was the only reason or price for Judas' betrayal of Jesus. I think it was **pride and arrogance.**

In fact, it is significant to me that Judas betrayed Jesus *immediately after Mary anointed him with the expensive perfume.* But that's a whole other teaching.

Speaking of pride and arrogance, there are some who feel that *everything and everybody has a price.* They want what others have ... without either the commitment, hard work, understanding or anointing to achieve it.

Consider the story of Simon from Samaria as recorded in Acts 8:14-23.

Peter and John were in Samaria ... they were laying hands on people and they were receiving the Holy Spirit.

A man named Simon pulled out his money and in Acts 8:19 says:

*"Sell me your secret! Show me how you did that! How much do you want? Name your price!"*

The next four verses give us Peter's response.

*"But Peter replied, 'May your money be destroyed with you for thinking God's gift can be bought! You can have no part in this, for your heart is not right with God. Repent of your wickedness and pray to the Lord. Perhaps he will forgive your evil thoughts, for I can see that you are full of bitter jealousy and are held captive by sin.'"*

This is one scripture that has been *misinterpreted by those who teach against prosperity*. "They" say that it's wrong to sow a seed just because someone is praying for you. "They" point out that you can't buy the gifts or favor of God and thus condemn those who ask people to sow seeds.

What "they" forget to point out is that Peter said to Simon in verse 21 as translated in the New Living Translation:

*"… You can have no part in this, for your heart is not right with God."*

Peter's objection to Simon was because *he didn't know God* … yet he was doing the things of God … in other words, *Simon wanted the gift without knowing the Giver*. **That doesn't work.**

157

God paid a very high price for you … salvation is not free … *it cost the life of His only begotten son, Jesus.*

1 Corinthians 7:23 in the New Living Translation says:

*"God paid a high price for you, so don't be enslaved by the world."*

The price that God paid for you also **washed away your sins**. Isaiah 44:22 in the New Living Translation says:

*"I have swept away your sins like a cloud. I have scattered your offenses like the morning mist. Oh, return to me, for I have paid the price to set you free."*

Child of God, I want you to be encouraged … you may feel like you're between a rock and a hard place … but God … that's right … *BUT GOD has a liberating word for you.*

Isaiah 43:1-3 in the Message Bible says:

*"Don't be afraid, I've redeemed you. I've called your name. You're mine. When you're in over your head, I'll be there with you. When you're in rough waters, you will not go down. When you're between a rock and a hard place, it won't be a dead end— Because I am God, your personal God, The Holy of Israel, your Savior. I paid a huge price for you … That's how much you mean to me! That's how much I love you! I'd sell*

*off the whole world to get you back, trade the creation just for you."*

Not only has God paid a high price … the ultimate price … it's *the most expensive price ever paid … for you.* Just remember …

*"… Don't be afraid, I've redeemed you. I've called your name. You're mine. When you're in over your head, I'll be there with you. When you're in rough waters, you will not go down. When you're between a rock and a hard place, it won't be a dead end— Because I am God, your personal God …"*

Then God said *"… I paid a huge price for you."*

One last observation … have you ever bought something even though you felt like the price might have been a little too high?

You were probably okay with your price as long as the item you purchased performed as expected.

Here's the question … **are you living your life worthy of the price God paid for you?** If not, why not? If not, *when are you going to start?*

Think about it.

"No one is useless in this world who lightens the burdens of another." Charles Dickens.

**Day
19**

# 21 Key Provisions of Your Benefits Package

**Does your job have benefits?**

Does your employer offer health care, 401K plans, paid-vacation days, sick days, holidays, flexible spending plans, child care, continuing education or other such benefits?

**The offer of health care will not benefit you unless you take advantage of it.**

Your 401K will never provide retirement income for you … unless you put something into it.

*The company child care facilities will be of little benefit to your children … unless you bring them to the facility.*

**Your employer can have the best benefits package in the world *but if you don't activate or participate in what is available to you* … then it will be of no real value to you.**

Basically, not using the benefits available … will have the same results as if they were not available to you at all.

Which brings me to a very important point:

As a child of God, you and I have the greatest benefit package ever put together. **This generous package of benefits is not the result of labor negotiations but rather a loving Father who wants the very best for you.**

Here are 21 key provisions of your personal benefits package.

## 1.    Recognize the origin of your benefits.

1 Corinthians 1:3 in the Message Bible says:

> *"May all the gifts and **benefits** that come from God our Father, and the Master, Jesus Christ, be yours."*

## 2.    The Author of all benefits wants you to have them.

2 Corinthians 1:1 in the Message Bible says:

> *"I, Paul, have been sent on a special mission by the Messiah, Jesus, planned by God himself. I write this to God's congregation in Corinth, and to believers all over Achaia province. May all the*

*gifts and **benefits** that come from God our Father and the Master, Jesus Christ, be yours! ..."*

## 3. Your benefits are beyond natural description.

1 Corinthians 2:9 in the Amplified Bible says:

*"But, on the contrary, as the Scripture says, What eye has not seen and ear has not heard and has not entered into the heart of man, [all that] God has prepared (made and keeps ready) for those who love Him [ who hold Him in affectionate reverence, promptly obeying Him and gratefully recognizing the **benefits** He has bestowed]."*

## 4. Keep His benefits foremost in your mind so you can claim them.

Psalm 103:2 in the New International Version says:

*"Praise the LORD, O my soul, and forget not all his **benefits**."*

## 5. Obedience brings benefits (i.e., Right associations bring benefits).

John 4:38 in the New International Version says:

*"I sent you to reap what you have not worked for. Others have done the hard work, and you*

*have reaped the **benefits** of their labor."*

## 6. A godly life benefits other believers.

Deuteronomy 18:7-8 in the New International Version says:

*"He may minister in the name of the LORD his God like all his fellow Levites who serve there in the presence of the LORD. He is to share equally in their **benefits**, even though he has received money from the sale of family possessions."*

## 7. Your benefits have a very real spiritual value.

Proverbs 8:12 in the Message Bible says:

*"I love those who love me; those who look for me find me. Wealth and Glory accompany me— also substantial Honor and a Good Name. My **benefits** are worth more than a big salary, even a very big salary; the returns on me exceed any imaginable bonus. You can find me on Righteous Road—that's where I walk— at the intersection of Justice Avenue, Handing out life to those who love me, filling their arms with life— armloads of life!"*

## 8. Sin obscures the value of your benefits.

Esther 5:13 in the Amplified Bible says:

*"Yet all this **benefits** me nothing as long as I see Mordecai the Jew sitting at the king's gate."*

## 9.    Neglect the Source and lose your benefits.

Deuteronomy 28:46-48 in the New Living Translation says:

*"These horrors will serve as a sign and warning among you and your descendants forever. If you do not serve the LORD your God with joy and enthusiasm for the abundant **benefits** you have received, you will serve your enemies whom the LORD will send against you. You will be left hungry, thirsty, naked, and lacking in everything. The LORD will put an iron yoke on your neck, oppressing you harshly until he has destroyed you."*

## 10.    Your actions activate or de-activate your benefits.

Proverbs 11:17 in the Amplified Bible says:

*"The merciful, kind, and generous man **benefits** himself [for his deeds return to bless him], but he who is cruel and callous [to the wants of others] brings on himself retribution."*

## 11.    Repentance brings His benefits.

Psalm 142:7 in the Young's Literal Translation says:

*"Bring forth from prison my soul to confess Thy name, The righteous do compass me about, When Thou conferrest **benefits** upon me!"*

## 12. Benefits encourage you during adversity.

2 Corinthians 4:1 in the Amplified Bible says:

*"THEREFORE, SINCE we do hold and engage in this ministry by the mercy of God [granting us favor, **benefits**, opportunities, and especially salvation], we do not get discouraged (spiritless and despondent with fear) or become faint with weariness and exhaustion."*

## 13. Spiritual blessings prompt natural benefits.

1 Corinthians 9:11 in the Amplified Bible says:

*"If we have sown [the seed of] spiritual good among you, [is it too] much if we reap from your material **benefits**?"*

## 14. Words fitly spoken bring benefits.

Proverbs 12:14 in the New Living Translation says:

*"Wise words bring many **benefits**, and hard work brings rewards."*

## 15. Living a righteous life brings immediate

**benefits.**

1 Timothy 4:8 in the New Living Translation says:

*"Physical training is good, but training for godliness is much better, promising **benefits** in this life and in the life to come."*

## 16.    How do you repay God for all your benefits?

Psalm 116:12 in the Amplified Bible says:

*"What shall I render to the Lord for all His **benefits** toward me? [How can I repay Him for all His bountiful dealings?]"*

## 17.    Praise God for His Benefits.

Psalm 13:6 in Young's Literal Translation says:

*"I do sing to Jehovah, For He hath conferred **benefits** upon me!"*

## 18.    Resting in the Lord brings His benefits.

Psalm 116:7 in Young's Literal Translation says:

*"Turn back, O my soul, to thy rest, For Jehovah hath conferred **benefits** on thee."*

## 19.    Meditating and living the Word brings benefits.

Psalm 119:16-17 in Young's Literal Translation says:

*"In Thy statutes I delight myself, I do not forget Thy word. Confer **benefits** on Thy servant, I live, and I keep Thy word."*

## 20. Giving increases your benefits.

Luke 6:38 in the Amplified Bible says:

*"Give, and [gifts] will be given to you; good measure, pressed down, shaken together, and running over, will they pour into [the pouch formed by] the bosom [of your robe and used as a bag]. For with the measure you deal out [with the measure you use when you confer **benefits** on others], it will be measured back to you."*

## 21. Benefits are manifested every day.

Psalm 68:19 says:

*"Blessed be the Lord, who daily loadeth us with **benefits**, even the God of our salvation. Selah."*

Child of God, now that's what I call an impressive benefits package … the best ever offered. However, *if you don't sign up for the package or participate in all that's available to you* … then you will never reap the rewards of this package.

If you have missed your opportunity in the past … start now.

**Day 20**

# 7 Ways to Prove You Are God's Favorite

Are you a planner?

*Are you the kind of person who prints out a MapQuest of the trips you take? Do you have your stops highlighted along the way?* Do you have the hotels confirmed?

*Are you the kind of person who plans your activities for tomorrow each evening before you go to sleep?*

**On your job ... do you utilize strategic planning in every assignment you're given?**

When your kids or grandkids are involved in sports or other extra-curricular activities ... *do you have a cooler with bottled water, sports drinks and healthy snacks?*

*Do you carefully plan family dinners for special events?*

*Are you one of those folks where everything has a*

*place and that's where it is when you need it?*

Were you able to say "yes" to any of the questions I just posed to you?

*If the answer is "yes" you take after your Father. I'm not necessarily talking about your earthly but rather your Heavenly Father.*

**God has always been a planner.**

I mean *God planned a supper 6,000 years before it happened*. That's what I call some **serious planning**.

Unfortunately, for many people, their *idea of **long-range planning** is whether or not to eat at **Denny's or IHOP** on Saturday morning*.

**And yes**, *the most important question*, shall we eat at 8 AM or 11 AM?

**Your success in life** … in your marriage … family … job … *investments will not just happen to you because you're a nice person or even because you love the Lord*. You **must have a plan**.

Proverbs 16:3 in one translation says:

> *"I commit my work to the Lord. My plans will succeed."*

**Each day is a gift to you** … what are your plans for this precious treasure of time *that God has given to* *you?*

Someone said once, **each day is a gift from God and what we do with that day is our gift to him**.

*Not only is God a planner ... but He knew you before you were ever formed in your mother's womb.*

Jeremiah 1:5 in the Amplified Bible says:

> *"Before I formed you in the womb I knew [and] approved of you [as My chosen instrument], and before you were born I separated and set you apart, consecrating you; [and] I appointed you as a prophet to the nations."*

If you've ever had any doubt that God has plans for you ... make sure you read, study and meditate on Jeremiah 29:11.

First, the King James Version says:

> *"'For I know the plans I have for you,' declares the LORD, 'plans to prosper you and not to harm you, plans to give you hope and a future.'"*

Second, the Message Bible Translations says:

> *"I know what I'm doing. I have it all planned out—plans to take care of you, not abandon you, plans to give you the future you hope for."*

Here are ... **seven ways to prove you're God's**

**favorite**.

**First, He knows the plans He has for you.**

*Plans can be good or bad depending on the heart of the one formulating the plans.* However, *there can never be a question about the kind of plans God would have for you.*

**Second, God's plan is to prosper you.**

When I read this verse, *I wonder how anyone could ever doubt whether or not God wants His children to be prosperous, successful and blessed.*

**If you're struggling from the quicksand of debt … that's not God's plan for you.**

*If you're so broke you can't "order it your way at Burger King" … that's not God's plan for you.*

*If you have to work two to three jobs just to make ends meet … that's not God's plan to prosper you.*

**Third, God will never make plans that are harmful to you in any way.**

*Being unable to sleep at night because you're worrying about where your next mortgage payment or rent check is coming from … is harmful to your health … so that can't be God's plan for you.*

*Tensing up with fear and dread every time the phone*

*or doorbell rings for fear of having to deal with a creditor ... is not God's plan for you.*

Proverbs 1:33 in the New Living Translation says:

*"But all who listen to me will live in peace, untroubled by fear of harm."*

## Fourth, God's plans are to give you hope.

When you're struggling to pay your bills, *worrying about the lack of good jobs*, or concerned about your health or that of a family member ... *hope is a wonderful thing.*

The very good news is God has a plan to give you hope ... *in everything you encounter.*

The scripture is clear ... hope comes from one place.

Psalm 62:5 in the New Century Version says:

*"I find rest in God; only he gives me hope."*

## Not only does He give you hope ... but it's how He gives it to you.

Romans 15:13 in the New Living Translation says:

*"I pray that the God who gives hope will fill you with much joy and peace while you trust in him. Then your hope will overflow by the power of the Holy Spirit."*

**Fifth, God will give you a future.**

The kind of future God is giving you … is not just eternal life.

I particularly like the New Living Translation of John 10:10 which says:

> *"The thief's purpose is to steal and kill and destroy. My purpose is to give them a rich and satisfying life."*

**Sixth, God knows what He's doing when it comes to you.**

The Message Bible Translation of Jeremiah 29:11 says:

> *"I know what I'm doing. I have it all planned out—plans to take care of you, not abandon you, plans to give you the future you hope for."*

I've had the privilege of knowing some really brilliant people. *I have discovered over the years that no matter how smart someone is … they occasionally make mistakes, albeit, good-intentioned ones.*

No matter how smart a person is … *either through intellectual acumen or common sense … they're still human and subject to making wrong decisions.*

However, ***God knows what He's doing and He's never made a mistake and never will.*** Not only that

… He will never abandon you in yours.

Hebrews 13:5 in the Amplified Bible says it this way:

> *"… for He [God] Himself has said, I will not in any way fail you nor give you up nor leave you without support. [I will] not,[I will] not, [I will] not in any degree leave you helpless nor forsake nor let [you] down relax My hold on you)! [Assuredly not!]."*

**Seventh, God will not only give you a future, He will give you the one you hoped for.**

Psalm 37:4 in the New Living Translation says:

> *"Take delight in the Lord, and he will give you your heart's desires."*

Not only will God give you the future you hope for … the desires of your heart … *He will ensure your personal success.*

Psalm 20:4 in the New Living Translation says:

> *"May he grant your heart's desires and make all your plans succeed."*

I think it's fair to say that considering these seven points and God's plans and promises for your future … you must be one of His favorites. I know I am.

I thought this teaching was complete … but then …

the Lord brought James 1:22-24 in the Message Bible to my remembrance. It says:

*"Don't fool yourself into thinking that you are a listener when you are anything but, letting the Word go in one ear and out the other. Act on what you hear! Those who hear and don't act are like those who glance in the mirror, walk away, and two minutes later have no idea who they are, what they look like."*

Today is your time to act on what you hear … and, yes, to know … **you're one of God's favorites**.

## Day 21

# 7 Reasons You Should Be Singing

I have a personal question for you.

**How's your singing?**

Do you sing primarily in the choir, *the pew* or the shower?

What kind of music do you sing … Christian … rhythm and blues … country and western … jazz … gospel … hip hop … pop … Christian?

Is your singing voice of a quality *that only a mother could enjoy?*

In days gone by, I said I sang "solos" … so low nobody could hear me. I've said I sing but nobody has ever asked me to make a music CD.

Those are things I have previously said … but no more. A fresh revelation of the last part of Mark 11:23 caused me to change the words coming out of my mouth.

> *"For verily I say unto you, That whosoever shall say unto this mountain, Be thou removed, and be thou cast into the sea; and shall not doubt in his heart,* __*but shall believe that those things which he saith shall come to pass; he shall have whatsoever he saith*__*."*

A further revelation came into my life when I scripturally understood the meaning of Psalm 95:1:

> *"O come, let us sing unto the LORD: let us make a joyful noise to the rock of our salvation."*

I used to joke about my "joyful noise." *The dictionary definition of noise added credit to my humor about my singing voice.* Dictionary.com defines *noise* as:

> **"sound, especially of a loud, harsh, or confused kind."**

Truthfully, I thought my singing sounded like ... a noise. However, *a fresh revelation into the scriptural meaning of* <u>*joyful noise*</u> *changed my thought pattern.*

According Strong's Concordance, the Greek word for joyful noise is ruwa` (ru aah) (H7321) and it means:

> **"to shout, raise a sound, cry out, give a**

**blast; to shout a war-cry or alarm of battle; to shout in triumph (over enemies); to shout in applause; to cry out in distress."**

In short, *a joyful noise is not a song but a shout*. And yes, a shout that should be done by everyone whether they have the five-octave range of Aaron Neville *or a voice like mine. We're supposed to shout in battle, in distress and in triumph.*

So everyone should be shouting and singing.

Let's go a little further with Colossians 3:16 in the Amplified *Bible which changed my perception and my reality about singing unto the Lord.* Colossians 3:16 in the Amplified Bible says:

*"Let the word [spoken by] Christ (the Messiah) have its home [in your hearts and minds] and dwell in you in [all its] richness, as you teach and admonish and train one another in all insight and intelligence and wisdom [in spiritual things, and as you sing] psalms and hymns and spiritual songs, making melody to God with [His] grace in your hearts."*

There are **seven reasons we should be singing to the Lord**.

## **First, the Word of God should have its home in our hearts and minds.**

The words spoken by God … and our Lord and Savior Jesus … *shall reign in our hearts.*

Luke 6:45 says:

> *"A good man out of the good treasure of his heart bringeth forth that which is good; and an evil man out of the evil treasure of his heart bringeth forth that which is evil: for of the abundance of the heart his mouth speaketh. We should be speaking the Words that Christ spoke."*

Proverbs 23:15 in the Message Bible says:

> *"Dear child, if you become wise, I'll be one happy parent. My heart will dance and sing to the tuneful truth you'll speak."*

## **Second, we should be teaching, admonishing and training others in the Word.**

This particular reason should be a no-brainer for every born-again believer … *if no other reason than the Great Commission.*

Matthew 28:19-20 says:

*"Go ye therefore, and teach all nations, baptizing them in the name of the Father, and of the Son, and of the Holy Ghost: Teaching them to observe all things whatsoever I have commanded you: and, lo, I am with you always, even unto the end of the world. Amen."*

Hebrews 5:12 in the New Living Translation actually sums things up when it says:

*"You have been believers so long now that you ought to be teaching others. Instead, you need someone to teach you again the basic things about God's Word ..."*

## Third, our teaching should contain insight, intelligence and wisdom.

This kind of teaching ... *is not based on your educational level or your intellectual prowess* but rather 1 Corinthians 2:16 in the Amplified Bible which says:

*"For who has known or understood the mind (the counsels and purposes) of the Lord so as to guide and instruct Him and give Him knowledge? But we have the mind of Christ (the*

*Messiah) and do hold the thoughts (feelings and purposes) of His heart."*

Thus far, we have learned that *EVERY BELIEVER should have the Word of God established in their hearts so they can teach and train everyone what they've learned with a wisdom beyond their natural minds.*

Now, *let's look again* at our primary text in Colossians 3:16 in the Amplified Bible which says:

*"Let the word [spoken by] Christ (the Messiah) have its home [in your hearts and minds] and dwell in you in [all its] richness, as you teach and admonish and train one another in all insight and intelligence and wisdom [in spiritual things, and as you sing] psalms and hymns and spiritual songs, making melody to God with [His] grace in your hearts."*

## **Fourth, we should sing psalms.**

According to Strong's Concordance the word psalms is (fall moss) psalmos (G5528) and it means:

**"a striking, twanging; of a striking the chords of a musical instrument; a psalm."**

Now I have to tell you that I started smiling when I saw "twanging" as it most often refers to country and western singers. So I guess the laugh is on everybody who's not into "twanging" ... because God wants us to be a "twanger."

1 Chronicles 16:9 says:

> *"Sing unto him, sing psalms unto him, talk ye of all his wondrous works."*

This particular scriptural admonition must be important to God *as the same verse is repeated ... word for word in Psalm 105:2.*

## **Fifth, we should sing hymns.**

According to Strong's Concordance the word for hymns found in Colossians 3:16 is the Greek word (who nas) hymnos (G5215) which means:

> **"a song in praise of gods, heroes, con-querors; a sacred song, hymn."**

*Does this definition of hymns line up with those you've been singing out of your church hymnal?* In most cases, I don't think so.

*We're to sing hymns of victory … over every foe.*
**Sixth, we should sing spiritual songs.**

There is a very specific direction in the scripture on the kinds of spiritual songs that we sing to Him.

> *"And they sang the song of Moses the servant of God and the song of the Lamb, saying, Mighty and marvelous are Your works, O Lord God the Omnipotent! Righteous (just) and true are Your ways, O Sovereign of the ages (King of the nations)!"*

**Seventh, we should be singing to God with grace in our heart.**

We're not just to sing to the Lord … *we're to sing with grace in a very specific manner.*

According to Strong's Concordance the Greek word for grace is (ha rus) charis (G5485) and it means:

> **"that which affords joy, pleasure, delight, sweetness, charm, loveliness: grace of speech; good will, lovingkindness, favour; benefit."**

Two final scriptures for your thought process: First,

let's look at Colossians 3:16 in the Message Bible which says:

*"Let the Word of Christ—the Message—have the run of the house. Give it plenty of room in your lives. Instruct and direct one another using good common sense. And sing, sing your hearts out to God!"*

There is a further confirmation of this teaching found in Ephesians 5:19:

*"Speak out to one another in psalms and hymns and spiritual songs, offering praise with voices [and instruments] and making melody with all your heart to the Lord."*

One last comment … let me hear you sing … me, me, me …

**Day 22**

# 7 Ways to Make a Good First Impression

Have you ever heard the expression ... *you only have one opportunity to make a good first impression?*

That's true. *I will tell you that you can't always judge a book by its cover ... but the look of that cover may keep me from ever finding out what's in the book.*

Here are seven keys to making a great Godly first impression.

## 1. Have Fun and Recognize Every Moment as an Opportunity

From *the time my feet hit the floor in the morning until my eyelids close at night ... I'm looking to rejoice in every moment and opportunity that God gives me ... and, by the way, have fun in the process.*

*My ability to have fun ... is not determined by the day of the week ... or even who I'm around.* I look for the humor in every situation because the scripture says in Proverbs 17:22:

*"A merry heart doeth good like a medicine: but a broken spirit drieth the bones."*

The Contemporary English Version of Proverbs 17:22 says:

*"If you are cheerful, you feel good; if you are sad, you hurt all over."*

Proverbs 17:22 in the Amplified Bible says:

*"A happy heart is good medicine and a cheerful mind works healing, but a broken spirit dries up the bones."*

Let's see … *if you're merry, cheerful and happy … then you're having fun in whatever you're doing.*

However, *if you're not having fun … then you're sad, hurting all over, with a broken spirit and sick.*

*I choose to have fun.*

## 2.    Smile … Let the Fruit Shine Through

Have you ever read an email telling you to smile if you want to be lazy because it takes fewer muscles to smile than frown?

I can recall a half dozen or more different totals on the muscles used to smile or frown. *In my research I found out that the medical opinions on the exact number of muscles to smile and/or frown … are as varied of the number of medically-approved diets.*

However, there is one consensus among the medical authorities. **It does take less muscles to smile than frown.**

However, I like the late great Louis Armstrong who sang:

*"When you're smilin' keep on smilin'. The whole world smiles with you."*

Here are *seven reasons why you should smile.*

### # 1 - You're uglier when you frown.

I have no scriptural basis for this reason … just the opinion of someone who has literally met hundreds of thousands of people in his life.

**Here's a revelation for you: <u>Even ugly people look better when they smile</u>.**

### # 2 - God smiles … so you should too.

Numbers 6:25 in the God's WORD translation says:

*"The Lord will smile on you and be kind to you."*

## # 3 - When you smile ... the Lord sends blessings your way.

Numbers 6:25-26 in the New Living Translation says:

*"May the Lord smile on you and be gracious to you. May the Lord show you his favor and give you his peace."*

## # 4 - When you smile ... mercy comes your way.

Psalm 31:16 in God's WORD translation says:

*"Smile on me. Save me with your mercy."*

## # 5 - God is smiling on you ... when you're learning His Word.

Psalm 119:135 in God's WORD translation says:

*"Smile on me, and teach me your laws."*

**# 6 - When you're down and out … God can make you smile again.**

Psalm 43:5 in The Living Bible says:

*"O my soul, why be so gloomy and discouraged? Trust in God! I shall again praise him for his wondrous help; he will make me smile again, for he is my God!"*

**# 7 - When you smile … favor is in your life.**

Psalm 67:1 in the New Living Translation says:

*"May God be merciful and bless us. May his face smile with favor on us."*

Smiling always creates a good first impression … and it's clear from scripture … that's what God wants you doing.

**3. Dress for Success**

**Rightly or wrongly, we often form an opinion of someone by the way they dress long before they ever open their mouths to speak.**

Years ago, I remember interviewing a young woman who scored *the highest score we had ever recorded on a typing and ten-key test*. It was *off the charts and with no errors … that's an absolute impossible to achieve ... but she did. The young woman was effi-cient and very attractive ... but I didn't hire her.*

The simple reason is that she was wearing a mini-shirt.

I knew that when the other women in that department saw an *attractive woman wearing a mini-shirt ... she would never be given a chance to survive. The fresh impression created by her dress would minimize her effectiveness ...* and I didn't hire her.

I felt bad about my decision ... and talked about it with my fine wife Bev. We called the young woman back in and explained the logic behind our decision. She was so appreciative as she was a single Mom with two small daughters.

This woman became one of the most efficient em-ployees we ever had. To this date, she is a *close fami-ly friend* who often *counsels women on how they should look when seeking employment. And by the way, she loves God with all her heart.*

However, the way she dressed ... almost cost her a job.

## 4.    Be on Time

*When someone is late ... they're sending you a mes-sage about themselves.* And, I will tell you it's a mes-sage *that doesn't convey a good or Godly first im-pression.*

*Being continually late reflects a lack of planning, a poor attitude, a lack of respect, a lack of organization and/or a lack of good habits.*

*When a person is late it's either a habitual or character problem.* Either way, it's not impressive.

**If a person does not value my time ... they do not value my life ... because my time is my life.**

## 5.    Listen

<u>*You will impress more people by your ability to listen than by the words you speak*</u>.

Everybody likes to have their opinion asked and valued.

If you want to make a good impression ... *listen for and remember* the name of every person you meet.

*The reason most people have difficulty remembering the names of the people they meet is because their focus is wrong.*

When the average person meets someone new ... they're focusing on *how they look, how they're being perceived* and *wondering whether or not they're making a good impression*.

Just relax ... when you meet a new person call them by name ... *several times during the conversation* ...

either orally or mentally. Repeat their name to yourself as they walk away.

If you learn to listen to the voice of the Holy Spirit ... *then you will automatically become a better listener in life.*

And by the way, **there is a lot more to listening ... than just waiting for your turn to talk**.

## 6.    Be Enthusiastic About Your Product

**If you don't believe in yourself or your product no one else ever will.**

*Selling ... whether it's widgets or the gospel ... is all about transference of feelings.*

If I can get you to feel about my product the way I feel about my product ... *you will buy or try my product.*

***You've got to be knowledgeable about your product ... you must be sold on your product ... if you ever want to sell it to anyone else.***

You must also be enthusiastic about your work ... whether it's secular or not.

Ephesians 6:7 in the New Living Translation says:

> *"Work with enthusiasm, as though you were working for the Lord rather than for people."*

## 7.    Don't Fake It … Be Genuine

The very first moment you meet someone is critically important.

**When you meet someone …** *as you shake their hand* **… they need to feel that at that very moment …** *they're the most important person in your life.* Because they are.

At the moment, you're shaking their hand … **you've made a conscious decision to spend that part of your life with them**. *They need to feel the importance that you assigning to this moment in time.*

Practice on looking directly into someone's eyes … *this lets the person know how deeply you value this moment.*

**The person that you're meeting or talking with needs to feel the sincerity of your heart.**

*When you practice these seven ways to make a good impression, <u>they will</u>.*

**Day 23**

# 7 Reasons Why You're a Genius

**You may be a genius *and you don't even know it.***

*While you may not qualify for membership in the Mensa Society whose members have an IQ of 130 and above … I believe you are a genius.*

*In fact, my definition of a genius is the same as Thomas Edison's, who had an IQ of 140.* He said:

### "Genius is one percent inspiration and ninety-nine percent perspiration."

*If you've got inspiration … with motivation and are willing to put up with a lot of perspiration … then in my book … you're a genius.*

Allow me to share seven reasons why you're a genius.

## 1.   Your DNA

You are a child of the most high God … you are child of a King … you are the offspring of the Master of the

Universe … the Creator of heaven and earth and all it contains.

You were made in His image and after His likeness.

Genesis 1:26 says:

> *"And God said, Let us make man in our image, after our likeness …"*

Let's make that verse personal.

> *"And God said, Let us make <<Your Name>> in our image, after our likeness …"*

Randy, Esther, Denise, Paul, Diane.

*My genealogy includes* … Abraham, Isaac and Jacob … *all multi-millionaires*. My genealogy also includes *Solomon, the wisest man of all times*.

My status … *my standing* … my DNA is further con-firmed through Galatians 3:29 which says:

> *"And if ye be Christ's, then are ye Abraham's seed, and heirs according to the promise."*

## 2. Your Mind

*If you are a Christian … even an imperfect Christian and I haven't met any other kind … you have the mind of Christ.*

I'm not making this up to make you feel good. It's the Word.

1 Corinthians 2:16 says:

*"For who hath known the mind of the Lord, that he may instruct him? but we have the mind of Christ."*

There are way *too many believers who sell them-selves short because they feel they're not smart enough.* That's just not the case ... if you believe the Word of God.

You have the mind of Christ and that makes you one of the smartest people around. *Now whether or not you choose to use that mind* ... is another question.

My prayer is that the mind of Christ would function ful-ly and freely within you *every moment of every day.* Is that your prayer too?

## 3. Your Common Sense

**If you're a genius *but you lack to ability to under-stand and communicate with people who aren't* ... your success in life will be limited.**

I happen to think people who demonstrate common sense on every level of life are in fact the real genius-es.

Common sense is defined by dictionary.com as:

**"sound practical judgment that is**

## independent of specialized knowledge, training"

*What's the origin of all wisdom and common sense?*

Proverbs 2:6 in the Contemporary English Version says:

> *"All wisdom comes from the LORD, and so do common sense and understanding."*

*God is no respecter of persons … what He gives to one … He gives to all. The difference is what we choose to do with what we have been given.*

Proverbs 3:13 in the Contemporary English Version says:

> *"God blesses everyone who has wisdom and common sense."*

The scripture is clear … **God expects us to use common sense**.

Luke 12:57 in the Message Bible says:

> *"You don't have to be a genius to understand these things. Just use your common sense …"*

When we're obedient to His direction … *using common sense* … we're successful.

Proverbs 8:14 in the New Living Translation says:

> *"Common sense and success belong to me. Insight and strength are mine."*

## 4.    Your Inspiration

*Do you have anybody in your life that inspires you …* perhaps a parent, a teacher, coach, best friend or business associate?

My fine wife, Bev, being number one … she always inspires me. *Grace, dignity, wisdom and spiritual balance.*

My parents have always been a source of inspiration … *to the extent they believe I can operate without limitation.*

Some are not as fortunate to have a loving spouse and highly supportive parents … but everybody has a constant source of inspiration … that's never wavered … never comes and goes … He's been rock steady … even before I made Him the Lord of my life.

John 1:14 AMP says:

> *"And the Word (Christ) became flesh (human, incarnate) and tabernacled (fixed His tent of flesh, lived awhile) among us …"*

2 Timothy 3:16-17 says:

*"All scripture is given by inspiration of God, and is profitable for doctrine, for reproof, for correction, for instruction in righteousness: That the man of God may be perfect, thoroughly furnished unto all good works."*

## 5.    Your Commitment

Some years ago, I heard the story of the chicken and the pig. A Pig and a Chicken were walking down the road.

The Chicken says, *"Hey Pig, I was thinking we should open a restaurant!"*

Pig replies, *"Hmmm, maybe, what would we call it?"*

The Chicken responds, *"How about Ham-n-Eggs?"*

The Pig thinks for a moment and says, *"No thanks. You only have to be involved ... but I'd be totally committed!"*

**God wants us focused on and totally committed to the instructions in His Word.**

Philippians 3:15-16 in the Message Bible says:

*"So let's keep focused on that goal, those of us who want everything God has for us. If any of you have something else in mind, something less than total commitment, God will clear your blurred vision—you'll see it yet! Now that we're*

*on the right track, let's stay on it."*

## 6.    Your Preparation

I personally think the greatest definition of genius was offered by Vince Lombardi, the legendary coach of the Green Bay Packers.

**"Plan your work and work your plan."**

God likes it when you plan your work and work your plan of commitment to His Kingdom.

Proverbs 21:5 in the New Living Translation says:

*"Good planning and hard work lead to prosperity, but hasty shortcuts lead to poverty."*

Through the scriptures we can see **where planning and preparing is important to God** ... if it's important to Him ... it had better be important to us.

Joshua 7:13 in the New Living Translation says:

*"Get up! Command the people to purify themselves in preparation for tomorrow. For this is what the Lord, the God of Israel, says: Hidden among you, O Israel, are things set apart for the Lord. You will never defeat your enemies until you remove these things from among you."*

Part of your daily preparation should be to sanctify yourself ... consecrate and yes, prepare yourself for what lies ahead.

**Your preparation needs to be blended with expectation.**

Joshua 3:5 says:

> *"For tomorrow, Jehovah will do wonders among you."*

One last thought, a part of preparation is planning. ***Do you have a plan for what you will do tomorrow?***

***If you don't have a plan for the day … the day will have a plan for you.***

**7.    Your Perspiration**

Thomas Edison, whom we quoted earlier, also said:

> **"Being busy does not always mean real work. The object of all work is production or accomplishment and to either of these ends there must be forethought, system, planning, intelligence, and honest purpose, as well as perspiration. Seeming to do is not doing."**

Genesis 3:19 says:

> *"In the sweat of thy face shalt thou eat bread, till thou return unto the ground; for out of it wast thou taken: for dust thou art, and unto dust shalt thou return."*

***Sweat equity came into being as a result of the sins of Adam and Eve.***

If you want to eat … to provide for your family … to succeed … you will need to sweat.

***When you work hard … you perspire … when you're under pressure … you sweat.***

Napoleon Hill, American self-help author, said:

> *"Patience, persistence and perspiration make an unbeatable combination for success."*

In my book … you possess the seven qualities required to be a genius.

Just one more thing.

*If you follow God … obeying His every instruction … that determines if you a true genius.*

# 7 Keys to Unlimited Success

**Day 24**

As a born-again Child of God … you have unlimited access to the *greatest, most generous and giving Benefactor ever.*

*Access is a privilege obtained through obedience and thankfulness.*

Here are seven ways to access His presence and power …

## 1.	Through the blood of Jesus.

Jesus was crucified … so through the shedding of His precious blood on Calvary's cross … *we could have access to the presence of God and the power of the Holy Spirit.*

Ephesians 2:18 in the New International Version says:

> *"For through him we both have access to the Father <u>by one Spirit</u>."*

One other scripture.

Romans 5:1-2 in the New International Version says:

> "Therefore, since we have been justified through faith, we have peace with God through our Lord Jesus Christ, <u>through whom we have gained access by faith into this grace in which we now stand</u>. And we rejoice in the hope of the glory of God."

**2.    Understand the parameters and possibilities of the access we've been given.**

Many may work at businesses where there are varying levels of access *to the same computer system*.

For instance, *we have a level for those who enter data.*

We have another level for those whose job description *requires them to create and analyze reports from the data that's entered.*

There is another level where certain employees not only have access to data entry and the creation of reports ... but *they also have the clearance to access all of our financial records.*

*You must have the proper access to do your job effectively.*

Galatians 4:7 in the Message Bible says:

> "Doesn't that privilege of intimate conversation with God make it plain that you are not a slave,

*but a child? And if you are a child, you're also an heir, with complete access to the inheritance."*

## 3. We have unlimited access to everything our Heavenly Father has.

The great news is that as a Child of God ... we have complete access to everything including our inheritance.

Matthew 16:19 in the Message Bible says:

*"And that's not all. You will have complete and free access to God's kingdom, <u>keys to open any and every door</u>: no more barriers between heaven and earth, earth and heaven. A yes on earth is yes in heaven. A no on earth is no in heaven."*

Hallelujah. You and I as born-again believers ... **"have complete and free access to God's Kingdom and keys to open any and every door ..."**

I personally recommend that you personalize this scripture and get it deep down into your spirit.

*"And that's not all. <<Your Name>> will have complete and free access to God's kingdom, keys to open any and every door: no more barriers between heaven and earth, earth and heaven. A yes on earth is yes in heaven. A no on earth is no in heaven."*

With that access *comes* His blessing flow and *power over every attack of the enemy.*

Matthew 16:19 in the New American Standard Bible says:

*"… I will give you the keys of the kingdom of heaven: and whatever you shall bind on the earth shall be bound in heaven: and whatever you shall loose on earth shall be loosed in heaven."*

**4.   Live in continual thanksgiving for the unlimited access we've received as a result of our obedience and faithfulness.**

1 Corinthians 1:4-6 in the Message Bible says:

*"Every time I think of you — and I think of you often! — I thank God for your lives of free and open access to God, given by Jesus. There's no end to what has happened in you — it's beyond speech, beyond knowledge."*

Having access to the King of Kings and the Lord of Lords *is not something to be taken lightly or for granted. We should be continually thanking God for all He has done and is doing for us.*

Psalm 35:28 in the Amplified Bible says:

*"And my tongue shall talk of Your righteousness, rightness, and justice, and of [my reasons for]*

*Your praise all the day long."*

## 5.     With unlimited access to the throne room of God … we're never alone.

1 Corinthians 4:7-8 in the Message Bible says:

> *"You already have all you need. You already have more access to God than you can handle. Without bringing either Apollos or me into it, you're sitting on top of the world — at least God's world — and we're right there, sitting alongside you!"*

One of my favorite scriptures is Deuteronomy 31:6 in the New Living Translation which says:

> *"So be strong and courageous! Do not be afraid and do not panic before them. For the Lord your God will personally go ahead of you. He will neither fail you nor abandon you."*

Psalm 139:5 in the Message Bible says:

> *"You know when I leave and when I get back; I'm never out of your sight. You know everything I'm going to say before I start the first sentence. I look behind me and you're there, then up ahead and you're there, too—your reassuring presence, coming and going. This is too much, too wonderful—I can't take it all in!"*

Hallelujah and Praise God for access.

**6.   If we fail to appreciate the access we've been given … we may find that we no longer have it.**

Ezekiel 44:13-14 in the Message Bible says:

*"They're fired from the priesthood. No longer will they come into my presence and take care of my holy things. No more access to The Holy Place! They'll have to live with what they've done, carry the shame of their vile and obscene lives. From now on, their job is to sweep up and run errands. That's it."*

Praising God for our access to Him is a choice … if we make the wrong choice … then we suffer the consequences.

Deuteronomy 48:47-48 in the New Living Translation says:

*"If you do not serve the Lord your God with joy and enthusiasm for the abundant benefits you have received, you will serve your enemies whom the Lord will send against you. You will be left hungry, thirsty, naked, and lacking in everything …"*

**7.   You need to understand how to gain favored access.**

Proverbs 18:16 in the New Living Translation says:

*"Giving a gift can open doors; it gives access to*

*important people!"*

I find the New Living Translation of the Hebrew text much more accurate than the King James Version which says:

*"A man's gift maketh room for him, and bringeth him before great men."*

Many leaders in ministry mistakenly teach that the gift referred to in Proverbs 18:16 is your natural abilities and what they perceive to be talent.

That sounds nice … but it's not what the Bible is saying or what the word gift means.

According to Strong's Concordance the word gift is the Hebrew word mattan (H4976) and it means:

**"gifts, offerings, presents."**

The word *mattan* appears in five verses according to the Hebrew Concordance of the King James Version and in each instance it's referring to a *monetary gift*.

At your convenience, I recommend you read Genesis 34:12; Numbers 18:11, Proverbs 19:6, Proverbs 21:14 and, of course, Proverbs 18:16.

It's clear the scripture is talking about a gift of financial value. The scripture is also clear that a financial gift will bring you before important and eminent people.

The Message Bible translation of Proverbs 18:16 says:

*"A gift gets attention; it buys the attention of eminent people."*

If you want access … and more importantly favored access … **you always bring a gift**.

**Day 25**

# 4 Places Not to Look for Answers and 7 Places to Find Wisdom

Proverbs 12:15 says:

*"The way of a fool is right in his own eyes, but he who listens to counsel is wise."*

Let me tell you four places *where you will rarely*, if ever, find the right answers or wisdom for living.

## 1. Friends without wisdom

If your friends are as lost as a goose in a blizzard *then the possibility of them offering you Godly wisdom is remote, at best.*

If your friend has held three jobs in the past two years … *they're not really the kind of expert you should be talking to when it comes to finding a new job or getting a promotion.*

In 1 Corinthians 5:11 the Amplified Bible says:

*"But now I write to you not to associate with any-*

*one who bears the name of [Christian] brother if he is known to be guilty of immorality or greed, or is an idolater [whose soul is devoted to any object that usurps the place of God], or is a person with a foul tongue [railing, abusing, reviling, slandering], or is a drunkard or a swindler or a robber. [No] you must not so much as eat with such a person."*

You also need to make sure that you're associating with people who can *encourage, exhort, edify and lift you up.*

Proverbs 13:20 in The Living Bible says:

*"Become wise by walking with the wise; hang out with fools and watch your life fall to pieces."*

## 2.    Talking heads on television

Walking the red carpet, *hosting your own television show or having Emmys or Oscars on your mantle doesn't automatically mean you know what you're talking about* or that you're an expert.

My Daddy … the greatest man I ever met … taught me years ago that *an expert is somebody fifteen miles out of town with a briefcase* or *it could be a drip under pressure.*

Compassionate conversation even when it's stained with tears *doesn't make you a competent counselor or an expert.* Jumping up and down *or dancing and shouting on the set of a TV show doesn't make some-one the pinnacle of wisdom.*

Proverbs 19:2 in the New Century Version says:

*"Enthusiasm without knowledge is not good. If you act too quickly, you might make a mistake."*

*I'm more interested in what the Word says than what Dr. Phil thinks.*

*The View I want of life … will never come from three argumentative women sitting on a couch but through the Father, the Son and the Holy Ghost.*

## 3.   Articles in secular magazines

If you want to be entertained and nauseous at the same time … walk slowly down the magazine aisle of your nearest grocery store observing the titles.

"Three Signs You Might Get Fired"

"The Ten Hottest Songs To Have Sex To"

"Eat Less, Exercise More … Blah Blah Blah"

"What Guys Really Fear About Cheating"

"6 Things You Didn't Know About Sweat"

If you look through these magazines … *you will notice in most instances advertisements offering products that will supposedly solve the kind of problems you just read about.*

When I read anything, it must pass the "Truth Test" administered by the Greater One that's within me.

## 4.    Google results on the net

Yes, you can find amazing, unbelievable information on the net. Type a few words in Google and voilà … a world of knowledge is before you.

I must, however, quickly point out that *any idiot with a computer and internet access can post their opinions about life or anything else.*

The results you find in a Google search should never be considered the truth … *the whole truth and nothing but the truth.* In fact, in many cases, the items you find have nothing to do with the truth.

John 14:6 says:

> *"Jesus saith unto him, I am the way, the truth, and the life: no man cometh unto the Father, but by me."*

Seek the Truth … Seek Him.

**Here are seven places where you should always look for wisdom.**

## 1.    Always look for wisdom from the One who

**is always right.**

Judges 18:5 says:

> *"And they said unto him, Ask counsel, we pray thee, of God, that we may know whether our way which we go shall be prosperous."*

## 2.  Always look for wisdom from someone who meets a scriptural criteria.

Psalm 1:1-2 in the Amplified Bible says:

> *"BLESSED (HAPPY, fortunate, prosperous, and enviable) is the man who walks and lives not in the counsel of the ungodly [following their advice, their plans and purposes], nor stands [submissive and inactive] in the path where sinners walk, nor sits down [to relax and rest] where the scornful [and the mockers] gather. But his delight and desire are in the law of the Lord, and on His law (the precepts, the instructions, the teachings of God) he habitually meditates (ponders and studies) by day and by night."*

## 3.  Always look for wisdom from someone who has a hunger to know more.

Proverbs 8:32-35 says:

> *"Now therefore hearken unto me, O ye children: for blessed are they that keep my ways. Hear instruction, and be wise, and refuse it not.*

*Blessed is the man that heareth me, watching daily at my gates, waiting at the posts of my doors. For whoso findeth me findeth life, and shall obtain favour of the LORD."*

The Message Bible translation says:

*"So, my dear friends, listen carefully; those who embrace these my ways are most blessed. Mark a life of discipline and live wisely; don't squander your precious life. Blessed the man, blessed the woman, who listens to me, awake and ready for me each morning, alert and responsive as I start my day's work. When you find me, you find life, real life, to say nothing of God's good pleasure. But if you wrong me, you damage your very soul; when you reject me, you're flirting with death."*

## 4. Always be willing to buy information that provides Godly wisdom.

Proverbs 23:22-23 says:

*"Hearken unto thy father that begat thee, and despise not thy mother when she is old. Buy the truth, and sell it not; also wisdom, and instruction, and understanding."*

The Message Bible translation says:

*"Listen with respect to the father who raised you, and when your mother grows old, don't neglect*

*her. Buy truth—don't sell it for love or money;
buy wisdom, buy education, buy insight."*

## 5.　Always seek an abundance of wisdom.

James 1:5 says:

*"If any of you lack wisdom, let him ask of God,
that giveth to all men liberally, and upbraideth
not; and it shall be given him."*

## 6.　Always know that wisdom will never contradict the Word of God.

Proverbs 19:2 in the New Century Version says:

*"Enthusiasm without knowledge is not good. If
you act too quickly, you might make a mistake."*

## 7.　Always look for wisdom to protect you.

Proverbs 2:9-11 in the New Living Translation says:

*"Then you will understand what is right, just, and
fair, and you will find the right way to go. For
wisdom will enter your heart, and knowledge will
fill you with joy. Wise choices will watch over
you. Understanding will keep you safe."*

It's also important to know that Godly wisdom *will often go against the flow of popular opinion or culture.*

Wisdom will often go against what's easy and *desira-*

*ble according to the standards of everybody else.*

The world's wisdom is to buy what you want when you want it ... without consideration for the consequences of tomorrow.

The good thing about wisdom is that it's not a re-specter of persons ... *everybody regardless of their socio-economic conditions can get wisdom* ... if they seek it.

**Wisdom is not hiding from you ... it's readily accessible.**

In fact, according to Proverbs 1:20 in the New Living Translation says:

> *"Wisdom shouts in the streets. She cries out in the public square."*

**When wisdom calls out to you ... answer and you will reap the reward.**

Proverbs 8:17-18 in the Amplified Bible says:

> *"I love those who love me, and those who seek me early and diligently shall find me. Riches and honor are with me, enduring wealth and right-eousness (uprightness in every area and rela-tion, and right standing with God)."*

I'd say ... that's a pretty good reason to be looking for wisdom in all the right places.

**Day**
**26**

# 10 Reasons to Be Ready to Read

**Read ... is the first four letters of ready.**

When you read His Word ... you're ready to understand that you're a *Child of God* and a *Joint Heir with Christ*.

When you read His Word ... you're ready to understand *why you need to be born-again.*

When you read His Word ... you're ready to know that God wants you to *prosper and be in health* just as your soul prospers.

When you read His Word ... you're ready to understand that God *not only forgives* your past sins ... He *forgets them* as well.

When you read His Word ... you're ready to experience *the good life God designed* for you.

When you read His Word ... you're ready to *defeat every attack* of the enemy.

When you read His Word … you're ready to *fulfill His plan for your life.*

God's Word contains the answers to every question you'll ever have *plus it gives you necessary instructions for living the good life.* It's your Owner's Manual and it explains in great detail *how to act and react to every problem that could possibly come your way.*

Let me quickly point out that *the enemy would like nothing better … than you choosing not to read … especially the Word of God.*

**The devil is the "author of illiteracy" … He does not want people reading the Bible.**

Every time you say you don't like to read … the sound you hear is the devil clapping for you.

I remember speaking in Baton Rouge, Louisiana, a number of years ago. In that meeting I was encouraging everyone to read whatever date of the month it was … that corresponding chapter in the Book of Proverbs.

For instance, on the first day of the month … you would read the first chapter of Proverbs. On the twenty-fifth day of the month … you would read the twenty-fifth chapter of Proverbs.

After the meeting a young man walked up to me and said, **"I don't like reading. What do you think about that?"**

I said, "First thing, you need to stop saying you don't like to read."

I asked him if he commuted to work and he said, yes, about thirty miles each way five days a week.

I asked him what he listened to … and he said, some gospel music. When I asked him what else he listened to … he reluctantly admitted that he also listened to some Hip Hop.

He said, "What do you think about that?"

I smiled and said: "I think you need to hop off of it."

There was another guy standing there who asked what I thought of country music.

I told him that if you played the song backwards you'd have a happy ending. *The man would get his dog back, his truck back and then his wife back.*

Summarizing … *if you don't like to read* … that's how you feel <u>at the moment</u>. **Stop saying it.**

Begin to listen to anointed teaching during your commute. If you *listen to the right teaching each day* … like those found on our Debt Free Army website … you will soon discover *you have a newfound desire to read*.

In searching the scriptures … I found the word "read" in the King James Version of the Bible a total of 66 times. Let's talk about journey through the Word to discover what the Word says about reading.

**First, when you read the Word … your first response … the right response is to do everything the Lord instructs you to do.**

Exodus 24:7 in the New International Version says:

> *"Then he took the Book of the Covenant and read it to the people. They responded, 'We will do everything the Lord has said; we will obey.'"*

**Second, you should read the Word of God every day … not just when you have a need or face an emergency … but every day of your life.**

Deuteronomy 17:19-20 in The Living Bible says:

> *"That copy of the laws shall be his constant companion. He must read from it every day of his life so that he will learn to respect the Lord his God by obeying all of his commands."*

**Third, reading the Word isn't just something you do in private … you should share the experience with those close to you.**

Joshua 8:34-35 in The Living Bible says:

> *"Joshua then read to them all of the statements of blessing and curses that Moses had written in the book of God's laws. Every commandment*

*Moses had ever given was read before the entire assembly, including the women and children and the foreigners who lived among the Israelis."*

**Fourth, reading the Word will help you avoid the consequences faced by others.**

2 Kings 22:15-20 in The Living Bible says:

*"Tell the man who sent you to me that I am going to destroy this city and its people, just as I stated in that book you read. For the people of Judah have thrown me aside and have worshiped other gods and have made me very angry; and my anger can't be stopped. But because you were sorry and concerned and humbled yourself before the Lord when you read the book and its warnings that this land would be cursed and become desolate, and because you have torn your clothing and wept before me in contrition, I will listen to your plea. The death of this nation will not occur until after you die-you will not see the evil that I will bring upon this place."*

**Fifth, reading the Word will tell you what to do when you're hungry.**

There are seasons where people need food stamps … or free food from a church or a neighbor but those measures should be temporary because your permanent solution is found in the scripture.

Matthew 12:3 in the New Living Translation says:

*"Jesus said to them, 'Haven't you read in the Scriptures what David did when he and his companions were hungry?'"*

**Sixth, reading was so important to Jesus that He was continually asking people if they had not read the Word.**

Matthew 22:31 says:

*"… have ye not read that which was spoken unto you by God, saying …"*

Mark 12:10 says:

*"And have ye not read this scripture …"*

Mark 12:26 says:

*"… have ye not read in the book of Moses …"*

**Seventh, reading the letters of the apostles, disciples and leaders brought encouragement to the early church much like reading good Christian books does today.**

Acts 15:31 in the Amplified Bible says:

*"And when they read it, the people rejoiced at the consolation and encouragement [it brought them]."*

**Eighth, reading will provide you insight and understanding on His plans for you.**

Ephesians 3:4 says:

> *"As you read what I have written, you will understand my insight into this plan regarding Christ."*

**Ninth, if you don't know how to read or simply don't bother … God is not happy with you.** Plus, a failure to read empowers the enemy's attacks in your life.

Isaiah 29:11-13 in the New Living Translation says:

> *"All the future events in this vision are like a sealed book to them. When you give it to those who can read, they will say, 'We can't read it because it is sealed.' When you give it to those who cannot read, they will say, 'We don't know how to read.' And so the Lord says, 'These people say they are mine. They honor me with their lips, but their hearts are far from me. And their worship of me is nothing but man-made rules learned by rote.'"*

I have a piece of free advice for everyone who has ever said … I don't like to read. STOP SAYING IT.

**Tenth, the only way you will ever be ready for or experience the power of God is by reading His Word.**

Matthew 22:29 in the New Living Translation says:

*"Jesus replied, 'Your mistake is that you don't know the Scriptures, and you don't know the power of God.'"*

Get READY to READ.

## More Than a
## Couple of Songs

"I'll be there" … is more than a song made popular by the Jackson 5 … *it's a statement that true friends* will say to each other *in times of adversity*.

**Have you ever had someone tell you they'll be there when you need them … only to look around when the occasion arises and no one is in sight?**

*Was the person close to you? Or someone that you previously thought was close to you? Was it somebody you have known for a long time? Was their absence in your need … due to the complexity of your problem or the fact they didn't want to get involved?*

**Did you ever need somebody to be in your corner … to speak up for you … *only to find their voice was silent when it really counted?***

<u>I have discovered in life that people have many acquaintances but few true friends</u>.

A friend is someone who will go down the road with you … *through the valleys of your life* and even on the self-directed detours *as you're trying to find happiness.*

I have several friends like that … one in particular that I'm thinking about. His name is Bob Mack from New Jersey. We've been friends for over half our lives. If the dictionary had pictures beside the words "true friend," there would be a picture of my buddy, Bobby Mack.

In tough times he's always been there. *I remember a particularly rough adversity in my life when I looked around to find he was the only friend still standing by me other than family.* It's sad that we live half a country away from each other.

But <u>I have another friend I'd like to tell you about …</u> <u>one who's close by and is *always there no matter* </u><u>*what I'm going through* … the good times … the challenging times (I refuse to have bad times)</u>.

In fact, Hebrews 7:25 in the Amplified Bible talks about this friend of mine. It says:

> *"Therefore He is able also to save to the uttermost (completely, perfectly, finally, and for all time and eternity) those who come to God through Him, since He is always living to make petition to God and intercede with Him and intervene for them."*

This friend not only can but He really wants to be there for me.

Not only that, but the scripture says *"… He is able also to save …"* me.

The Greek word for save is sozo (G4982) which means:

**"to save, keep safe and sound, to rescue from danger or destruction, to make whole."**

According to Strong's Concordance, the Greek word sozo is used a total of 118 times in 103 verses in the King James Version of the Bible.

One prominent Bible dictionary defines sozo as …

**"-saved: The word 'save' in the original Greek is sozo and means: 'safe' or, 'in a state of being saved from things which make you unsound' (examples being, destructive ideas and philosophies held, poverty, etc.), 'to do well', 'to keep safe and sound', 'to rescue from danger and adversity', 'to make whole', 'to restore to health', to' preserve', etc."**

Vines Bible Dictionary says that sozo is *"inclusively for all the benefits bestowed by God on man in Christ."*

**You've got benefits as well.**

So it's clear that *when Jesus saves you …* it *means*

*much more than just providing you with a first class ticket to heaven.*

Jesus is saving you from sin, sickness, disease and poverty ... now as well as in eternity.

Hebrews 7:25 says:

> *"Wherefore he is able also to save them to the uttermost that come unto God by him ..."*

John 14:16 in the New International Version says:

> *"Jesus answered, 'I am the way and the truth and the life. No one comes to the Father except through me.'"*

**Jesus is ever making intercession on our behalf with our Heavenly Father ... that means every minute of every day.**

The Message Bible translation of Hebrews 7:25 says:

> *"He's there from now to eternity to save everyone who comes to God through him, always on the job to speak up for them."*

Child of God, are you seeing this?

<u>*Jesus is on the job ever ready to speak to God on our behalf whenever we need it*</u>.

**When we need an advocate ... He's there on our**

**behalf. We will never have to worry about Him showing up.** The Contemporary English Version says He *"lives"* to speak up for us.

<u>Even when we mess up … He's there by our side … Jesus is not a fair-weather friend</u>.

Proverbs 18:24 in the Amplified Bible says:

> *"The man of many friends [a friend of all the world] will prove himself a bad friend, but there is a friend who sticks closer than a brother."*

**Not only do you have a friend that's closer to you than any family could ever be … He always answers when you call** … no busy signals … no answering machine … no voice mail … no pager number … *no "Can I call you back … I'm on another call?" response* … just His private line … and He's ready to listen and help.

Psalm 86:5 says:

> *"For thou, Lord, art good, and ready to forgive; and plenteous in mercy unto all them that call upon thee."*

We know that God is good … many of us have been taught that since the day we were born. Others, like my fine wife, were adults when they first experienced the love of our Lord.

*<u>We know that He is ready to forgive … but He will only</u>*

*do so when we ask*.

We know or should know ... even if we need to be reminded ... that **we can call upon Him in difficult times, filled with desperate circumstances, and He'll be there.**

Psalm 96:6 says:

> *"Give ear, O LORD, unto my prayer; and attend to the voice of my supplications."*

**Now here's the really good news ...**

Psalm 86:5-7 says:

> *"In the day of my trouble I will call upon thee: for thou wilt answer me."*

This scripture says that if you call upon Him He will answer you. **The scripture doesn't say ... He might answer you** ... it doesn't say ... He'll think about answering you if it's convenient ... *no, the scripture is clear* ... if you call upon Him, He will answer you.

Psalm 86:7 in the Message Bible says:

> *"Every time I'm in trouble I call on you, confident that you'll answer."*

If He answers every time we call ... then I'm prompted to ask each of us a question.

## How much of God do we want?

Way too many believers treat our Heavenly Father as "iGod."

If you own and/or are familiar with iPhones, iPads, iPods or any other smart phone or tablet that has touchscreen technology, then you understand this frame of reference.

On the modern electronic gizmos … when you want something, you lightly touch the screen and you've got it.

Way too many Christians treat God the very same way … as iGod … only touching Him with an iGod kind of experience.

The late great singer Ella Fitzgerald had a song titled *All of Me.*

I feel prompted to share the only part of the song that comes to my mind.

**"All of me, why not take all of me? Can't you see I'm not good without you?"**

Earlier I asked, "How much of God do you want?" The real question is how much of you does God want? The answer is simple: *All of you.*

And yes, He wants to bless you … to meet your every need … but He wants you to desire more than anything else to be in His presence.

Remember …

**Jesus is always there for us … working on our behalf and that's something we can always count on … no matter what.**

# Day 28

# 7 Ways God Wants You to Multiply

**God wants to multiply everything … in our lives.**

Deuteronomy 8:13 in the Amplified Bible says:

> *"And when your herds and flocks multiply and your silver and gold is multiplied and all you have is multiplied."*

Can somebody say, "Hallelujah!!"

Here are seven ways God wants you to multiply.

**First, multiplication can take place even while you're facing adversity.**

The early church started growing daily … after the Day of Pentecost … when the persecution started … they separated and multiplied … that's Kingdom math.

Acts 6:7 in the Amplified Bible says:

> *"And the message of God kept on spreading, and the number of disciples multiplied greatly in*

*Jerusalem; and [besides] a large number of the priests were obedient to the faith [in Jesus as the Messiah, through Whom is obtained eternal salvation in the kingdom of God]."*

Acts 9:31 gives us the secret to church growth.

*"Then had the churches rest throughout all Judaea and Galilee and Samaria, and were edified; and walking in the fear of the Lord, and in the comfort of the Holy Ghost, were multiplied."*

The Message Bible translation of Acts 9:31 says:

*"Things calmed down after that and the church had smooth sailing for a while. All over the country—Judea, Samaria, Galilee—the church grew. They were permeated with a deep sense of reverence for God. The Holy Spirit was with them, strengthening them. They prospered wonderfully."*

*As they were obedient to His principles and percepts ... multiplication took place through His Word.*

Acts 9:24 says:

*"But the word of God grew and multiplied."*

The Message Bible translation of Acts 9:24 says:

*"Meanwhile, the ministry of God's Word grew by leaps and bounds."*

**Second, God can multiply what you've got while everyone around you is decreasing.**

Psalm 107:38 says:

> *"He blesses them also, so that they are multiplied greatly, and allows not their cattle to decrease."*

**Third, God wants to multiply the days of our lives.**

Proverbs 9:11 in the Amplified Bible says:

> *"For by me [Wisdom from God] your days shall be multiplied, and the years of your life shall be increased."*

Hallelujah!!!

God wants to multiply the length of our lives through His wisdom … *which is His Word*. Knowledge of His Word will multiply the number of days that we have on planet earth.

Proverbs 9:11 in the New Living Translation says:

> *"Wisdom will multiply your days and add years to your life."*

**Fourth, God can multiply peace in your life … regardless of who is in power.**

Daniel 4:1 in the Amplified Bible says:

> *"NEBUCHADNEZZAR THE king, to all people, nations, and languages that dwell on all the earth: May peace be multiplied to you!"*

You can have grace and peace multiplied in your daily life regardless of which political party is in power. Our peace is not dependent on politics and world events.

Delight on the words found in 2 Peter 1:2 which says:

> *"Grace and peace be multiplied unto you through the knowledge of God, and of Jesus our Lord."*

The Amplified Bible version of 2 Peter 1:4 says:

> *"May grace (God's favor) and peace (which is perfect well-being, all necessary good, all spiritual prosperity, and freedom from fears and agitating passions and moral conflicts) be multiplied to you in [the full, personal, precise, and correct] knowledge of God and of Jesus our Lord."*

**Fifth, never forget who brought multiplication into your life.**

Hosea 4:7 in the Amplified Bible says:

> *"The more they increased and multiplied [in prosperity and power], the more they sinned against Me; I will change their glory into shame."*

When we seek Him … *God will show us many, many visions of the things He will manifest in our lives.*

Hosea 12:10 in the Amplified Bible says:

*"I have also spoken to [you by] the prophets, and I have multiplied visions [for you] and [have appealed to you] through parables acted out by the prophets."*

**Sixth, the fruit of the spirit will be multiplied in your life.**

Jude 1:2 in the Amplified Bible says:

*"May mercy, [soul] peace, and love be multiplied to you."*

**Seventh and finally, God will multiply our personal relationship with Him.**

2 Peter 1:2 in the Amplified Bible says:

*"May grace (God's favor) and peace (which is perfect well-being, all necessary good, all spiritual prosperity, and freedom from fears and agitating passions and moral conflicts) be multiplied to you in [the full, personal, precise, and correct] knowledge of God and of Jesus our Lord."*

Now let's go a little further …

Matthew 14:16-20 says:

*"But Jesus said unto them, They need not de-*

*part; give ye them to eat. And they say unto him, We have here but five loaves, and two fishes. He said, Bring them hither to me. And he commanded the multitude to sit down on the grass, and took the five loaves, and the two fishes, and looking up to heaven, he blessed, and brake, and gave the loaves to his disciples, and the disciples to the multitude. And they did all eat, and were filled: and they took up of the fragments that remained twelve baskets full."*

Every time I read this passage of scripture, I'm reminded of a very powerful message the Lord gave me … never to be hypnotized by the appearance of lack … but that's a teaching for another day.

***Several things I want us to see in this scripture:***

Matthew 14:19 says:

*"And he commanded the multitude to sit down on the grass …"*

**First, Jesus brought order to the situation … and that's what we need to do.**

If you're in financial trouble right now … you need to bring order to your situation.

Have you ever seen a movie, TV program or experience in real life … a situation where someone loses their job … and their house becomes a wreck … looks like it was hit by an internal tsunami … that's the worst thing a person can do ...

Order never comes out of chaos. *Discipline deter-mines your direction.*

**Second, He started with what He had** ... five loaves and two fishes. This little boy didn't just run through Long John Silver's ... he had very expensive fish.

We need to start where we are with what we've got.

Matthew 14:16 says:

> *"They have no need to go away: give ye them to eat. We have enough to eat and plenty to share."*

No matter how deep your debt ... or intense your despair ... you have everything God requires to have your needs met *and plenty to spare and share with others.* It is interesting to note what the disciples wanted to do to the hungry people ... *"send the multitudes away ..."*

When you take what you have ... give it to God and ask Him to bless it, break it and multiply it ... you are taking your problem of insufficiency out of the natural realm and releasing it to the supernatural for a solution ...

When we release what we have to God for Him to bless it ... we are opening the door for supernatural increase.

The scripture is clear … if you do this … then God will do that.

Mark 10:29 in the Message Bible says:

> *"Jesus said, 'Mark my words, no one who sacrifices house, brothers, sisters, mother, father, children, land—whatever—because of me and the Message will lose out. They'll get it all back, but multiplied many times in homes, brothers, sisters, mothers, children, and land—but also in troubles. And then the bonus of eternal life! This is once again the Great Reversal: Many who are first will end up last, and the last first.'"*

Too many believers think we will only get Heavenly rewards … but Luke 18:29 in the Message Bible translation says:

> *"'Yes,' said Jesus, 'and you won't regret it. No one who has sacrificed home, spouse, brothers and sisters, parents, children—whatever—will lose out. It will all come back multiplied many times over in your lifetime. And then the bonus of eternal life!'"*

**Day 29**

## Let's Talk About Lust

Have you ever read a verse *when suddenly you received a totally different interpretation of what it means ...* or what the Lord wanted you to get from it on a particular day?

I remember the day a fresh revelation came to me as I was reading Galatians 5:16:

> *"This I say then, Walk in the Spirit, and ye shall not fulfil the lust of the flesh."*

I first heard this Galatians verse taught as a "quit quit" and "don't don't" verse. In other words, *live a godly life by not going to movies*, watching television, dancing, smoking, drinking, looking at girls or *anything that doesn't happen within the four walls of the church.*

The verse says: *"... you shall not fulfil the lust of the flesh."*

The word fulfill is the Greek word teleo (G5055) and it means:

**"to bring to a close, to finish, to end, to pay."**

In the Strong's Concordance the Greek word (G1939) for lust means:

**"desire, craving, longing, desire for what is forbidden, lust."**

Way too many believers get into financial trouble because they desire things *which they perceive to be ...* soul satisfying and life fulfilling *... simply because others have them ... or these "things" will somehow meet a need for them.*

The Greek word for *lust* is mentioned 38 times in 37 verses according to the Hebrew Concordance of the King James Bible.

As I began to read those verses ... I felt stirred to discuss the first one on the list which is Mark 4:19:

*"And the cares of this world, and the deceitfulness of riches, and the lusts of other things entering in, choke the word, and it becometh unfruitful."*

**It's not that God is opposed to us having things ... *but rather the things having us.***

For years, I've taught that prosperity is not what you have ... prosperity is what has you.

Does securing the things of this world ... the newest cars, toys, electronic gadgets, clothes, shoes, things ... *take the place of your desiring, craving and longing for the Word of God* ... the things of God ... the presence of God?

**How do people get into financial trouble?**

They buy things they don't need ... *with money they don't have* ... to impress others or *fulfill something they feel is missing in their own lives.*

The Amplified Bible translation of Mark 4:19 offers a clearer perspective on what this verse actually means.

> *"Then the cares and anxieties of the world and distractions of the age, and the pleasure and delight and false glamour and deceitfulness of riches, and the craving and passionate desire for other things creep in and choke and suffocate the Word, and it becomes fruitless."*

What becomes fruitless?

***God's Word working within us.***

What is a distraction of this age?

In my opinion, *it's <u>anything that separates us from what should be our first love</u>, the Word of God and our relationship with our Heavenly Father.*

Depending upon the season of our lives ... as children grow up ... *they begin to drive and hang out with their friends.* They begin to spend more time with others than they do with us.

*How do you feel when you aren't needed as much?*

How did you feel when your opinion wasn't as valued as it used to be?

*How did you feel when you only had a few minutes here and there* talking with your children?

How do you feel about your children making choices *that don't reflect or respect the things that you've taught them?*

**Have you ever had your home treated more like a bed and breakfast?** That's where your children stayed in the same room … ate your food … but otherwise were off visiting places or out with their friends?

Don't get me wrong … there is a natural progression in childhood development.

*You just want your children to remember the instructions … the values that you've taught them from an early age … and let's be real … **to still be needed in their lives other than when there's a problem or emergency**.*

Now … **can you imagine how our Heavenly Father feels about us?** How we've ordered our priorities and *treated Him in our daily lives?*

Let's go a little further. Mark 4:19 also warns us about *"… the pleasure and delight and false glamour … the craving and passionate desire for other things …"*

I find "false glamour" to be an interesting phrase.

**Have you ever seen advertisers use anyone ugly in television commercials?**

Have you ever wondered why?

It's simple … **advertising executives know they're selling an illusion of what your life would be like if you buy their product**. The advertisers' desire is to paint a pleasing picture in your mind … *one beyond a reality that you're currently experiencing … and they know that ugly won't do it.*

The advertisers' end-game is for you to crave and passionately desire the products they're promoting … **to the extent that you'll do whatever is necessary (including the bondage of debt) to possess them**. They are feeding on needy people.

**What is the consequence of yielding to the allure of the advertisers?**

The last few words of Mark 4:19 gives us a real warning when it says:

> *"… the craving and passionate desire for other things creep in and choke and suffocate the Word, and it becomes fruitless."*

*Our desire … our lust for things … will choke and suf-*

*focate the Word.* Pay particular attention to the scripture when it says that the Word will become *"fruitless."*

Sadly, that means that the Word of God is not first in your life … *that the promises of the Word … the benefits of Sonship that He promised you … will not be reproducing fruit in your life.*

In fact, you will experience crop failure in epic proportions.

**The lost of this world are searching for what is missing in their lives … Jesus!** They look to the world because they know no other place to go. But as Christians we not only have the answer for self-fulfillment, *it is our duty to share it with others and rescue them from this demonic deception and not fall into it ourselves.*

God has made amazing promises to us in His Word … *but if we let fleshly desire for other things and people take precedence over Him … then we're going to live an unfulfilled and disappointing life and be no better off than those who have no God.*

The Message Bible translation of Mark 4:18-19 sums it up pretty good when it says:

*"The seed cast in the weeds represents the ones who hear the kingdom news but are overwhelmed with worries about all the things they have to do and all the things they want to get. The stress strangles what they heard, and noth-*

*ing comes of it."*

Being consumed by the things you want to get … *the things you want to do and the people you want to spend time with* … other than God … *means you're committing mental suicide by choking the very life out of yourself and your dreams.*

It doesn't matter how many sermons you've heard … how many seminars you've attended or how much Christian TV you've watched … **misplaced spiritual priorities permit financial and personal stress to take root in your life.**

As the verse says: *"The stress strangles what they heard, and nothing comes of it."*

That's why we should follow the advice found in Galatians 5:16. The Amplified Bible translation says it this way:

> *"But I say, walk and live [habitually] in the [Holy] Spirit [responsive to and controlled and guided by the Spirit]; then you will certainly not gratify the cravings and desires of the flesh (of human nature without God)."*

When it comes to living a fulfilled, fruitful and godly life … it's not so much what we stop doing as it is what we start doing.

**We must develop the habit of walking, living, being totally responsive to and guided by the Holy**

Spirit ... *then everything else will fall into place.* *It's a matter of putting the Word of God to work in our lives.*

**Day
30**

# 7 Things God Told Me About More Money

**MORE MONEY!**

I'm not trying to be prophetic, pre-sumptuous or provocative … *but there are times in our lives when we need more money.*

**God showed me seven principles we can follow when we are praying for money.** These principles are *good guidelines* in which to *check our motives and actions.*

God wants us blessed … *no question about that.*

God wants us prosperous … *that's what the Word says.*

God's best for His children *never includes anyone living* in the bondage of debt *and the agony of lack.* That anyone includes YOU.

**Our greatest desire should be for His wisdom, grace, salvation, presence, peace, joy and right-eousness.**

That being said, *there are times when we simply need more money.*

Hebrews 4:16 says:

> *"Let us therefore come boldly unto the throne of grace that we may obtain mercy, and find grace to help in time of need."*

The Amplified Bible translation of Hebrews 4:16 says:

> *"Let us then fearlessly and confidently and boldly draw near to the throne of grace (the throne of God's unmerited favor to us sinners), that we may receive mercy [for our failures] and find grace to help in good time for every need [appropriate help and well-timed help, coming just when we need it]."*

Here are **seven things told me about bringing more money into our lives.**

**1. There can be no conscious sin in our heart or head.**

Psalm 66:18 says:

> *"If I regard iniquity in my heart, the Lord will not hear me."*

Notice the Word says "regard" iniquity ... that means *considering it or holding it close.*

The Message Bible translation of Psalm 66:18 puts it this way:

> *"If I had been cozy with evil, the Lord would never have listened."*

If you have *asked forgiveness for a wrong-doing, don't let the devil beat you up over it*. <u>God forgives AND forgets; it's the devil who likes to remind you of your past</u>.

But equally important … don't you be reminding yourself about sins from your past.

**2. Realize that He is with you 24/7.**

Psalm 139:3-4 in the New Living Translation says:

> *"You see me when I travel and when I rest at home. You know everything I do. You know what I am going to say even before I say it, Lord."*

**As I said a couple of days ago … God always answers when our call** … *no busy signals* … no answering machine *… no voice mail* … no pager number … *no "Can I call you back … I'm on another call?" response … just His private line* … and He's ready to listen and help.

**3. Plan your days to fulfill His calling upon your life.**

Psalm 19:2 says:

> *"Day unto day uttereth speech, and night unto night sheweth knowledge."*

The Contemporary English Version of Psalm 19:2 says:

> *"Each day informs the following day; each night announces to the next."*

Before you go to sleep tonight … **create a to-do list of the things you plan to accomplish the next day.**

List them by priorities based on your goals in the six major areas of your life … spiritual, family, financial, physical, mental and social. **Make them specific with an assigned time line and priority.**

## 4. Live a righteous life.

Psalm 24:3-4 says:

> *"Who shall ascend into the hill of the LORD? or who shall stand in his holy place? He that hath clean hands, and a pure heart; who hath not lifted up his soul unto vanity, nor sworn deceitfully."*

The New Living Translation of 1 Peter 1:15 says:

> *"But now you must be holy in everything you do …"*

*How do you know what to do … it's simple … do what the Word says.*

*A righteous life is a continual search for His presence and the revelation of His Word.*

*When you want His Word and His presence more than anything else*, then you're getting closer to the righteous life.

## 5. Follow His instructions for living your daily life.

Psalm 15:1-5 in the Amplified Bible says:

> *"LORD, WHO <u>shall dwell</u> [temporarily] in Your tabernacle? Who shall dwell [permanently] on Your holy hill? <u>He who walks and lives uprightly and blamelessly</u>, who works rightness and justice and <u>speaks and thinks the truth in his heart</u>, He who does not slander with his tongue, nor does evil to his friend, nor takes up a reproach against his neighbor; In whose eyes a vile person is despised, <u>but he who honors those who fear the Lord</u> (<u>who revere and worship Him</u>); who swears to his own hurt and does not change; [He who] <u>does not put out his money for interest</u> [<u>to one of his own people</u>] and who will not take a bribe against the innocent. <u>He who does these things shall never be moved</u>."*

## 6. Don't engage in mental or sexual lust, fornication or adultery.

1 Thessalonians 4:3 in the Amplified Bible says:

> *"For this is the will of God, that you should be consecrated (separated and set apart for pure and holy living): that you should abstain and shrink from all sexual vice."*

What TV shows do you watch? Do you have the movie channels which typically glorify things ... God doesn't? What about movies?

What do you think when an attractive and perhaps provocatively dressed woman walks by or a muscular man catches your eye?

Think about these things ... search your heart.

## 7. Give your tithes and offerings—they unlock the windows of God's bank.

Malachi 3:10 says:

> *"Bring ye all the tithes into the storehouse, that there may be meat in mine house, and prove me now herewith, saith the LORD of hosts, if I will not open you the windows of heaven, and pour you out a blessing, that there shall not be room enough to receive it."*

The Message Bible translation of Malachi 3:10 says:

> *"Bring your full tithe to the Temple treasury so that there will be ample provisions in my Temple.*

*Test me in this and see if I don't open up heaven itself to you and pour out blessings beyond your wildest dreams."*

We tend to get into financial trouble and out of the will of God due to the CIA. I'm not talking about the Central Intelligence Agency but rather three things that feed our selfish desires … **C**onvenience … **I**ndulgence … **A**ppearance.

We get in debt for convenience: *"My life would be easier if I had that new chain saw, [dishwasher], [car]."* **Convenience is an excuse for justifying debt to make your life easier.**

Indulgence gets people into debt because they feel they *deserve a new dress [golf club], [dinner out] because they had a hard day at the office.* **Indulgence is an excuse for trying to make yourself feel better by spending money.**

The debt trap of appearance is *being more concerned about what others are thinking than what God's Word says.* **Our security must come from God and not in thinking we must have the latest "everything" to live a satisfied life.**

James 4:3 says:

*"Ye ask, and receive not, because ye ask amiss, that ye may consume it upon your lusts."*

The word lusts is defined as **"desires for pleasures."**

It's the Greek word hēdonē (H2237). This particular word is mentioned 5 times in the Greek concordance of the King James Version of the Bible.

The Contemporary English Version of James 4:3 says:

> *"Yet even when you do pray, your prayers are not answered, because you pray just for selfish reasons."*

There are dozens of verses that point out how God wants you blessed financially, but we must never forget why He blesses us.

As the scripture clearly says, *"we're blessed to be a blessing."*

God doesn't want you broke and living in lack, *but He wants you to monitor your priorities and seek first His righteousness*.

Matthew 6:33 says:

> *"But seek ye first the kingdom of God, and his righteousness; and all these things shall be added unto you."*

**There is one final thing I feel led to say ... be prepared to receive money from a totally unexpected source.**

That's what He told me to say today.

**Day 31**

## One Plus One Equals One

**Do we believe words are important to God?**

Do we believe that every one of the 800,000 words in the Bible is *strategically placed to benefit those who love Him?*

Do we believe that *when God says something He means it* even if we don't understand every word?

Do we believe the words in the Bible offer us a *roadmap for enjoying and experiencing the good life* … the God kind of life?

Do we believe that the *collective wisdom in the Word of God is far more insightful* than every book on marriage and finances ever written?

I trust you said "yes" to all of the previous questions. If not, *you may need a spiritual check-up from the neck-up.*

The reason for these questions is this … I was stirred, troubled and provoked this morning as I was reading in the Word.

Mark 10:7-8 says:

> *"For this cause shall a man leave his father and mother, and cleave to his wife; And they twain shall be one flesh: so then they are no more twain, but one flesh."*

Verse eight in the Amplified Bible says:

> *"And the two shall become one flesh, so that they are no longer two, but one flesh."*

Let's look at one more translation … verse eight in the Message Bible says:

> *"Because of this, a man leaves father and mother, and in marriage he becomes one flesh with a woman—no longer two individuals, but forming a new unity."*

When a man and a woman get married … and let me be clear … **marriage is supposed to be between a man and a woman**. PERIOD. PARAGRAPH. To think otherwise is an insult to God's creation and a clear indication that the person declaring it is not familiar with scripture. Romans 1:24-27 is a good start for the doubters.

Back to the teaching … **marriage is between a man and a woman and according to the scripture … one plus one equals one**. The husband and wife joined together in holy matrimony become one flesh … a unity … the symbol of One.

The meaning of "one" in Mark 10:8 has the same meaning as "one" in Mark 12:29 even though they are translated from different Greek words … they are both translated as "one."

Mark 12:29 says:

> *"And Jesus answered him, The first of all the commandments is, Hear, O Israel; The Lord our God is one Lord."*

For the purpose of discussion … I think we can agree that *"one" means "one."*

I also think it's important for us to consider Mark 10:9 in the Amplified Bible which says:

> *"What therefore God has united (joined together), let not man separate or divide."*

Let me make one other point … I had not planned on teaching about this subject but I was clearly directed of the Lord to do so.

I do have one request before proceeding … *please read this entire teaching before finalizing your opinion.* (Smiling.)

In the 21st century, it has become fashionable and often "recommended" by financial experts that couples have "his" and "her" checking accounts. **The logic is simple … what's mine is mine and what's yours is yours.** But that is like saying … ***marriage doesn't***

**mean you have to share everything**.

I have had couples tell me that it makes life easier for them.

To me, **it simply means the couples have taken the first step toward separation whether financial or legal**.

When couples have separate checking accounts … it means there a part of "my" life that's being withheld from "your" life even though we agreed to be one flesh.

Let me quickly say that I do recognize that some *spouses are spiritual knuckleheads as well as being financially illiterate*.

I recognize that some spouses are against tithing and giving offerings … and that the *only way the other spouse can do either is if they maintain a separate checking account*.

I also recognize that some people are married to spouses that *are inconsiderate, if not deceptive, when it comes to money*.

I recognize that some spouses *will never talk with their spouse about finances and money matters*.

While I recognize all these things … *I still think God somehow took this into account when He divinely in-spired every single word in the scripture*. It may take a little more prayer and effort, but the Word has to be doable or it wouldn't be in the Bible.

And God's certainly not caught off guard by the antics of the 21st century husband and wife.

**Facts change.** *Truth remains truth.* Sometimes living in truth is not easy but that doesn't minimize the fact *that truth is truth.*

If you have separate checking accounts, it's basically saying I don't trust my spouse. **Separate checking accounts allow a spouse to hide expenses and basically "do their own thing" just as they did when they were single.** Are you single or married? That is the question.

Whether knowingly or unknowingly, separate checking accounts also send a message that questions whether or not the marriage is solid.

Let me quickly add that *the husband should not be dictatorial when it comes to the checkbook and financial decisions ... but neither should the wife.*

Whoever controls the checkbook ... should remember that you are "one" with your spouse. **The same is true with the budget and/or family spending plan. It's the two of you working together on one plan.** *Not I'll do my thing and you do yours.*

The bottom line of marriage is that "we're in this together" ... it takes both of you to make it happen.

**Each spouse should have access to the check book, debit card and cash.**

Both spouses should know about all the investments, insurance policies and estate plans. There are three primary things that wives fear in a martial relationship.

**Debt, Divorce and Death.**

**If a man loves his wife ... then he should want her as knowledgeable as possible and prepared for any eventuality.**

If spouses are openly discussing the family's financial situation ... it lessens the possibility of confusion.

I think spouses should agree that any purchase over a certain amount has to be agreed to by both ... *I don't care who "brings home the bacon." And it should not be a matter of one badgering the other to get their way.* The "do unto others" scripture is well applicable here.

**I consider the family contributions of a stay-at-home Mom to be as significant and her job just as demanding as that of any man.** The pressure points may be different but stress is stress ... regardless of how you characterize it.

I also think that couples should have *extensive and truthful financial conversations before they ever say "I do."*

There should never be any financial surprises waiting for newlyweds after the honeymoon. Personally, **I see nothing wrong with asking to see your intended's credit bureau file before you get married.**

I suggested that to a couple once and both thought it was too personal. **When you marry someone – their credit score directly affects your entire life—how personal is that?**

Marriage is about intimacy and personal knowledge of and with your spouse.

If one partner is unwilling to share a credit bureau file … then it makes me wonder if they're hiding something. I've heard way too many horror stories about spouses who hid undisclosed debt and financial obligations until after the wedding. What a way to start a marriage.

You've got to ask yourself … why would somebody do that … unless their motivation is deceitful? It's better to bare your finances before your bodies … or you're exposing yourself to heartache.

Mark 10:8 in the Message Bible says:

> *"… no longer two individuals, but forming a new unity."*

How can there possibly be unity in a marriage if you're both leading separate financial lives?

You've got a choice … follow the world or follow the Word. I've made my choice.

# RichThoughts for Breakfast

## Volume 7

## Invite Harold Herring to speak at your church, event, or rally.

Would you like to invite Harold to be a guest speaker at your church, event, or rally? Just send an email to:

**booking@haroldherring.com**

**or call 1-800-583-2963**

With a mix of humor, practical strategies, and Biblical insight Harold will inspire, encourage, and prepare you to change your financial destiny and set you on the path to not only set you free from debt but keep you free of debt and living the debt free life God has called you to.

Keep Thinking Rich Thoughts,

*Harold Herring*

# RichThoughts for Breakfast

## *Jump Start Your Day!!*

This motivating start to your day is something no one should be without. I guarantee you will be glad you called in.

*Harold Herring*

### 712-432-0900
Access Code 832936#

**Playback Daily Call**

712-432-0990

Access Code 832936#

*The call starts at 8:30 AM EST seven days a week.*

**Practical Strategies, Biblical Insights and
Thought-Provoking Humor**

These are just a few of the things you are missing
if you're not joining us every day for the
**RichThoughts for Breakfast** morning call.

**Get Ready to be Inspired, Encouraged, and Entertained.**

*Your Rich Thoughts are your leap to your future success!*